The Small Business:
Lessons from Minority Business Owners

DR. M. T. BAKARI

DEDICATION

I dedicate this book to the twenty business owners in Newport News,
Virginia, who took time out of their busy daily schedules to contribute their
voices to my work. Each of them willingly shared their perspectives, and I
thank them. My hope is that each person will remain steadfast in his or her
entrepreneurial journey. I also dedicate this work to my husband Harvey,
my parents, and my four children who have been a constant inspiration.
Thanks to all of you..

CONTENTS

PREFACE

The information in this book is based on actual research conducted in Newport News, Virginia. Newport News is a city in southeast Virginia with a large racial minority population, according to the U.S. Census Bureau. Census data shows that in 2012, 51% of the city's residents were minorities. Despite the high minority population, census data also showed that only 3.5% of the city's minorities own businesses. The mismatch between the large minority population and the small number of businesses owned by this segment of the city's population was indicative of a slow-growing, or stagnant, minority business sector. The disparities between minority business ownership and minority population are stark. National data from the Census Bureau showed the racial minority population is 22.3%, and this segment of the population owns 22.1% of active businesses. Annually, these enterprises contribute over $1.2 trillion to the economy. In Virginia, where this researcher originated, this information of was sufficient concern to the states' leaders that the Council on Virginia's Future, a state-sponsored accountability organization, agreed that overall business creation in Newport News was lower than in other Virginia cities.

The reason for the study that preceded this book was to determine how African American micro-enterprise owners coped with barriers and business structures that affected business initialization, growth, and success. Exploration of this problem was from the experiential perspectives of the micro-business owners. Ultimately, the results of my investigation apply broadly to minorities.

1
URBAN MINORITY BUSINESS

"Discriminatory practices consume the time, talent, and energies of both perpetrators and victims, and block opportunities for capable individuals and companies to make the maximum possible contribution to both society and the economy." – Shelton, 2010

Micro-entrepreneurs pursued business ownership for a variety of reasons. Barriers hindered the development of their micro-enterprises and altered how these entrepreneurs coped with the challenges of business ownership. The identified barriers included discrimination, information asymmetry, capitalization limitations, inconsistent regulatory enforcement, and administrative delays. They reported having difficulty acquiring or accessing the resources they needed to develop and execute strategic plans. Despite the existence of these and other barriers, micro-entrepreneurs persevered, sought new knowledge through networking, shared business strategies, supported one another, mentored nascent and aspiring entrepreneurs, and served their community. There is renewed awareness of the challenges faced by Minority entrepreneurs. The information contained in this book provides anecdotal evidence and insights that stakeholders may use to strengthen resources, affect policy changes, enhance management strategies, and promote economic vitality.

The chapters in this book are purposely short. Annoying details that researchers often include in their writings were simplified, and the relevant facts included. When I took on this challenge, I wrote from the perspective of a consultant. I hope to open your mind to the breadth of the problem and offer some solutions or pathways of avoidance.

Most cities in the United States are racially diverse communities where minorities account for a high percentage of each city's population. The minority population can consist of any combination of African-Americans, West Indians, Hispanics or Latinos, Asians, and small percentages of Native Americans and Pacific Islanders.

In spite of the racial diversity of this country's cities, why is it that only 7.1% of African-Americans nationwide actually own or operate businesses? Based on calculations made by government statisticians from 2010 census records, business participation across all races in this country, Whites and Asians have higher business participation rates than African Americans and Hispanics. This is the general trend. An even bigger problem is that the revenues generated from all minority businesses mirror the population percentages.

It is a known fact, and it is widely understood that anyone starting a business will encounter obstacles. Researchers, city managers, and proponents of business development have focused a little attention on the particular problems that minorities face during business startup. For example, when labor market forces disenfranchise a minority, and that person cannot find a new job, few direct support mechanisms offer retraining or education for self-employment. Furthermore, these mechanisms might be inaccessible. To develop practical solutions, investigation of the minority business experience in cities across the nation must be continuous. That is, if researchers, cities' leaders, and legislators hope to gain an understanding of the particular challenges faced by minorities with respect to business start-up. Precise identification of the problems minorities encounter is crucial to policy developers, to future generations of minority entrepreneurs, to the effectiveness of business development initiatives, and economic growth at the local level..

2
THE BIG QUESTION

This book is based on a single, central question: What are the difficulties or barriers associated business start-up for minorities? Of course, this might seem overly simplistic, but it is a start. This fundamental question leads to other issues. Are there differences between how minorities approach business? What specific skills or knowledge do minority business owners need to meet these challenges? What government and social agencies are involved? Moreover, how can these agencies better help minority entrepreneurs?

Promising and ambitious minorities encounter difficulties when starting their businesses, yet social and commercial systems do not adequately support the development these enterprises. In cities where more and more residents are racial minorities, recent census data shows that less than 10% of any given city's minorities own businesses; the exception to this is Asians. It is understood that small businesses fuel local economies, generate jobs, and contribute to the social well-being of communities. The low rate of minority business engagement in cities across this country demonstrates the need for identifying obstacles to business creation, and the need for solutions to those impediments. The problem is that racial minority entrepreneurs do not get adequate business advice, assistance, training, or educational support to overcome non-economic barriers to business development. Specifically, the problem is the impact of existing business and social structures on business activity among
minorities in urban areas..

3
UNDERSTANDING THE DYNAMIC

The reason for studying the transactional difficulties associated with starting a business is to dig deep into individuals' stories of and look at the problem from the experiential perspective of minorities. The remainder of the information in this book came from scholars and college student-researchers who conducted experiments and investigations. For a detail list of these sources, see the Resources section at the back of the book. In academic research, there are two key elements that explain how the research was done – the research method and the research design. First, the research method; the qualitative method was used here. This means that the information collected was not numerical (no quantitative analysis was used); all information came directly from business owners who had been in business for more than five years. Each of the twenty people interviewed recalled their personal experiences and shared their stories with me, the investigator. The second element that explains how this research was done is known as the research design. I chose a phenomenological research design; I used this design because there was an identifiable trend here (a phenomenon), and I could not find any academic, or high-quality information that focused on the minority micro-business in this city.

According to most dictionaries, a phenomenon is an event or occurrence that is observable; in this case, business ownership among minority groups has been a longstanding problem to which we have no solution. Phenomenological research design captures the elements of the phenomenon. This design allows the researcher to record and describe the lived experiences, perceptions, and recollections of people through the narratives, observation, or living alongside individuals to explore their life events. This research design is ideal for human science research. Through

4

data collection, using a verifiable interpretative technique, utilization of software, this study provided accurate, fact-filled, and timely information about the difficulties associated with business startup as perceived by the minority entrepreneurs I interviewed.

Awareness of the transactional difficulties experienced during the startup phase, and identifying which structures or agencies could facilitate the startup process, would lay the groundwork for actionable steps to solving the problem of low levels of business participation among racial minorities. I purposefully sought out twenty minority business owners who could identify and discuss the difficulties they encountered while setting up their businesses. The business owners recalled their experiences and told their stories in recorded interviews.

The stories of the twenty people who contributed to my original research and to this book have the potential to change the institutional support dynamic for minority small business. Particularly in terms of reducing or eliminating barriers and difficulties, improving education and training programs, and enhancing policies and business development initiatives. Without a clear understanding of the challenges faced by minorities, and without complete awareness of barriers that slow or deter minority entrepreneurs during the critical startup phase of business development, solutions to the problems will not be forthcoming.

A Short Discussion of Motivation

Psychoanalysis is way outside the boundaries of my expertise. That said, a little understanding of the mind of the entrepreneur can go a long way toward envisioning his or her world view. The topic of motivation was ubiquitous in   investigations of the entrepreneur. Motivation was part of the human psyche that involved principles, feelings, and reasoning. The human psyche produced motivators that drove individuals over the threshold of business conceptualization, on toward venture start-up. Scholars and researchers defined motivations as driving forces or factors that compelled the entrepreneur to combine knowledge, assets, and resources to build profit-producing enterprises. This definition mirrored Schumpeter's description of what the entrepreneur was. Moreover, entrepreneurial motivation flowed from two directions, pull factors, and push factors. Theorists conceptualized motivational factors as part of the management decision matrix; one set of conditions drove (pushed) individuals to act, and a different set of conditions incentivized (pulled) individuals to pursue a goal. The committed entrepreneur was a product of these antagonistic motivational forces.

In studies published in 2009 and 2010, researchers explored the factors influencing entrepreneurial motivation. Three general topics emerged from these quantitative and qualitative studies. First, the reasons for pursuing entrepreneurship varied from person to person and from one environment to another. Second, negative, or extrinsic factors such as personal life issues (divorce, workplace problems, low wage employment, underemployment, and unemployment) triggered a survival mechanism impelling people to become entrepreneurs. Third, positive intrinsic factors including wealth creation, independence, autonomy, and upward mobility encouraged people to take risks to achieve prosperity. Ultimately, the entrepreneurs' motives were self-interest or the need for achievement. To date, studies focused on entrepreneurial intentions, cognition, and behavior proved the hypothesis that motivation was singularly causative in the decision to become self-employed. Similarly, researchers' efforts to determine entrepreneurial personality characteristics led to the general conclusion that there was little difference between entrepreneurs and managers in terms of optimal characteristics. Goals, aspirations, and intentions were part of the motivation complex that resulted in entrepreneurial action. Based on their meta-analysis, these scholars proposed a redirection of research efforts toward investigating the complexities of entrepreneurial motivation and behavior.

Researchers systematically tested the motivations, business strategies, and community resources of African American entrepreneurs. In these types of studies, researchers found intrinsic motivators such as self-reliance, the desire for wealth, and gaining respect were psychological drivers for African Americans. Using statistical data collected from 1997 to 2002, researchers confirmed a 45% increase in African American business ownership. Researchers further investigated the differences in entrepreneurial motivation between African Americans and European Americans and found no difference between the two groups. However, researchers could not explain the increased rate of business startups among African Americans.

4
THE SCHOLARS' VIEW OF MINORITY BUSINESS

Few investigators devoted efforts to holistically studying minority entrepreneurs in particular environments. For many years, and primarily by looking at historical facts, and using census or local level data, investigators narrowly focused their research. The different areas studied included single ethnic groups, gender comparisons, entrepreneurial outcomes, measures of entrepreneurship, and entrepreneurial characteristics. There continues to be disagreement, argument, and dispute in entrepreneurship research arena because most researchers use an intra-disciplinary approach (this is like looking through colored glass, everything is going to have the same hue). Experts in psychology, sociology, management, and economics, individually contributed to the growing body of literature. Recently, some researchers advocated for a multi-disciplinary approach as a way to combine knowledge from various views. One scholar emphasized the need for researchers to consider an inter-disciplinary approach, claiming that there was a tendency to overestimate internal entrepreneurial factors and underestimate the influences of external factors. In other words, it is time to take the blinders off; nothing happens in isolation. Perhaps research is often too narrow. While the inter-disciplinary approach has the potential to bring complexity to the research process, it could result in higher quality information, and in developing solutions to these complex problems.

Based on the inter-disciplinary recommendation, the following discussions incorporate historical, philosophical, and interdisciplinary discoveries to form a panoramic view of the minority business experience. This is a presentation of concepts (what researchers discovered) and interpretations linked to the minority business owners' and entrepreneurs' experiences. There are three parts to this discussion. Firstly, there is a general discussion of the entrepreneur and society. Secondly, there is an explanation of the two theories that framed my investigation. Lastly, there is a discussion of minority entrepreneurs, with individual studies of African Americans, West Indians, Hispanics, and Asians.

The Entrepreneur and Society

This conversation must begin with defining the differences between an entrepreneur and a business owner. So far, the two terms have been used interchangeably, but that is not exactly correct. Joseph A. Schumpeter was a political scientist and economist in the early part of the 20th century. After immigrating to the United States, he became a Harvard professor. He defined modern entrepreneurship and developed the economic theories that formed the basis for entrepreneurship research as it is today. Joseph Schumpeter's writings were originally published in 1934. Within his writings, this Harvard professor developed a definition of what the entrepreneur was; and, researchers who came after Schumpeter used their own disciplinary expertise to explaining how the entrepreneur functioned in various environments. From numerous studies during the past century and into the 21st, scholars and researchers claimed that individuals selected one of three paths to entrepreneurship. First was the economic opportunity path, along which entrepreneurs established enterprises that relied on particular markets and market forces. Twentieth-century researchers created the building blocks for understanding the entrepreneur and entrepreneurship by clarifying and modernizing Joseph Schumpeter's definitions.

So let us revisit Professor Schumpeter's theory for a moment. According to the professor, the principle of entrepreneurship argued that entrepreneurs fuel a nation's economy. Entrepreneurs contributed to communities by using available resources, investing time and effort, and taking risks. Considering the definition of what the entrepreneur accomplished, one can find considerable research that explains how people functioned in various environments, markets, and industries.

The contributions of entrepreneurs to the world's societies were frequently acknowledged in the literature. Irrespective of the path taken to achieve entrepreneurship, entrepreneurs fueled the economies of nations around the world. Historical records and evidence from archeological excavations in the Middle East proved that entrepreneurial principles advanced from economic practices developed in Mesopotamia during the Bronze Age. According to Landes, Mokyr, and Baumol, who wrote The Invention of Enterprise: Entrepreneurship from Ancient Mesopotamia to Modern Times, the economic transformations of Mycenaean Greece and surrounding societies around 1200 BC, were made through entrepreneurship. African hieroglyphics celebrated the entrepreneur, confirming that entrepreneurship developed rapidly during a power shift when the Egyptian government was at its weakest. These authors developed two propositions through their research. First, the entrepreneur was born to seize the opportunity, and second, the phenomenon of business ownership was inextricable from its history.

Researchers repeatedly showed the interaction between government policy and the entrepreneur. In 2001, Paul Burns wrote Entrepreneurship and Small Business. Paul Burns looked at entrepreneurship through the ages and showed how King James and the Crusaders used policy to maintain Muslim communities for local economic stability in the 14th century. Reflecting on the history of the Middle Ages, Burns emphasized the need for continuous policy development to increase businesses' contributions to societies in the modern era. Robert Weems wrote Business in Black and White, in 2010. In this book, he reinforced the role of government by drawing on 20th and 21st century examples of legislators' policy attempts to stimulate and encourage the growth of minority businesses. Alongside these notable books, researchers and scholars underscored the need for policy alignment with the entrepreneur, confirming the vital role of entrepreneurial education and the development of entrepreneurial competencies to prepare societies for the future. Researchers also agreed that government support of business ownership and self-employment both have coexistent benefits.

Robert Weems gave several examples of legislative efforts to spur business development in minority communities. From President Calvin Coolidge to President Barack Obama, government policies targeted minority neighborhoods, business owners, and enterprises to stimulate self-employment, economic growth, and job creation. For example, the Community Reinvestment Act of 1977 was designed by legislators to assist minorities in low-income communities; this was a notable example of targeted government policy. The Community Reinvestment Act was to initiate urban development through business ownership, reduce persistent poverty, reduce unemployment, and lessen the adverse impact of poverty on broader economic growth. The key argument here is that for a community to engage and prosper from entrepreneurial activity, understanding the structures of existence of the business owners was requisite to creating an optimal blend of talent, function, and economic vitality.

5
MINORITY DISADVANTAGES

An early 20th century German, Max Weber wrote essays on sociology, economics, and politics; Weber's writings were macro-analytic (broad analysis including many variables) and remained relevant through the 20th century. In one of Max Weber's well-known passages, there was an expression of the state of scholarly perspective, that is, how scholar-researchers viewed the condition of the world. According to Max Weber, scholars and social scientists analyzed all events through the lens of "racial qualities," (for more details, read The Methodology of Social Sciences, 2011, p. 69). Weber believed, or perhaps hoped, that eventually, scholars would set aside their racial preconceptions and move toward pragmatism.

One of the key business theories that came out of Max Weber's work was the opportunity structure theory. The opportunity structure of society is an explanation of how people's access to occupations and resources is set up to support people achieving their goals and supporting their way of life. This social theory is centered on the fact that external elements (frameworks within a given society) can empower or impede individual progress. Moreover, social structures lend to the individual's capability to be upwardly mobile and to the manipulation of socioeconomic forces that stagnate the advancement of groups in our society. The disadvantage theory was a subset of the opportunity structure theory.

The disadvantage theory of entrepreneurship, developed by Dr. Ivan Light in the late 1970s, became the preponderant approach used in research to study African American and other minority business owners. The emphasis was focused on analyzing the socio-cultural patterns of discrimination and disadvantage. Researchers expanded their investigations to include examining how these forces restricted access to the resources and assets necessary for business development. Dr. Light was a proponent of the cultural thesis of entrepreneurship. This scholar expanded the concept that differences in entrepreneurial capabilities were race-based, and that culture created the problems that individual members experienced in the business environment. Examples of the cultural hypothesis included the legacy of slavery, social individualism, lack of business solidarity, and poor networking among some groups.

One of Dr. Light's discoveries was that as global industrialism expanded, so too did the number minority-owned businesses, but that was not the case in the United States. The uniqueness of the relationship between American industrialism and minority business ownership was baffling, so researchers continued to search for a sociological explanation of why racial minorities in the United States had not achieved the same levels of business ownership and self-employment as ethnic minorities in developed nations in Europe. Dr. Light's groundbreaking work on the disadvantage theory of entrepreneurship received endorsements and critiques from researchers over the last several decades.

For a moment, consider the arguments between some scholars and Dr. Light's view of African Americans. Although Dr. Light's analysis was plausible, there are scholars who claim that some of the earlier researchers were remiss and had not fully considered the 300 years of blocked social mobility endured by African Americans. Researchers who disputed the disadvantage theory challenged the supposition that the internal culture of African Americans was singularly responsible for the challenges facing this group of entrepreneurs. They proposed instead that societal forces erected substantial institutional barriers that prohibited entrepreneurial development. After examining the historical documentation of African American entrepreneurship, scholars provided context and validation for the argument that national culture was a key contributor to low levels of minority business ownership, especially for the African American business owner.

Scholars and researchers used historical viewpoints to explain how barriers limited entrepreneurial growth. In these investigations, researchers determined that discriminatory barriers block minority entrepreneurs in four different ways. First, there were barriers restricting access to startup and working funds. Second, there were barriers limiting access to education, skill development, and training. Third, there were barriers restricting and reducing the size of businesses; and fourth, these barriers potentiated and/or hastened business failure. Researchers determined low rates of ethnic minority entrepreneurial participation resulted in economic inefficiency, little innovation, slow job creation, and diminished productivity. Deep-seated discriminatory attitudes and exclusionary business practices marginalized and restricted the size of ethnic minority businesses, slowed business growth rates, and limited ethnic minority businesses to competitive, labor-intensive industries like janitorial services, hair salons and barber shops, and landscaping services.

The disadvantage theory suggested that minorities chose alternative paths to upward social mobility because of forces within the labor market. Forces within the labor market discriminated against minorities, disenfranchised them, rejected them, and often left these people unemployed. Under the framework of the disadvantaged theory, researchers found that minorities who encountered social discrimination, low wages, and rejections from within the labor force often turned to or were pushed into, self-employment and business ownership. When researchers explored ethnocultural, financial, managerial, psycho-behavioral, and institutional challenges that minorities encountered in the workplace and the business environment, three central concepts emerged. First, for the minority worker, low wages and failure to advance within a company was caused by the managers or leaders who held the preconceived notion that the minority's contribution to the company was limited by language barriers, unrecognized education or training credentials, and failure to assimilate to the organization's internal structure. Second, financial uncertainty pushed minorities into self-employment. Moreover, the organization often discredited the innovative contributions made by the minority employee. Finally, through the process of reverse-assimilation, minority innovations were woven and adopted by the company as its own.

One researcher suggested that, out of the fundamental human need to survive, minorities pursued self-employment and business ownership as a direct result of disproportionate discrimination within the labor market. According to other researchers who held a similar view, labor market discrimination affected minorities differently, and disproportionately channeled minorities into poorer quality jobs. For peoples with dark skin, African Americans, Africans, and West Indians, racial discrimination resulted in lower rates of employment, lower wages, and exclusion from advancement. Legal and social movements had eliminated overt forms of discrimination in America, but subtle discriminations continued to plague minorities within the labor force.

Socio-economic theorists found that entrepreneurial development, when it occurred at the local level, created stability, and sustainability within communities affected by economic downturns. Researchers also found that low levels of business had toxic effects on the rate of a community's economic development. Society had a genuine interest in promoting minority business ownership because increased levels of business ownership potentially reduced poverty, reduced social problems, reduced dependency on the dole, and stabilized unemployment. Furthermore, promoting entrepreneurship contributed to economic growth, and balanced income and social inequities.

Scholars developed two theories to explain the economic effect of unemployment and the subsequent changes in self-employment - approaches that reflected positively on the disadvantage theory. Some researchers postulated that unemployment resulted in a net increase in self-employment because would-be business owners pursued self-employment out of necessity. Secondly, the self-employed created jobs through the acts of business ownership and business growth efforts; consequentially, there was a net decrease in unemployment. Minority entrepreneurs contributed to lower levels of unemployment because their self-employment reduced competition for jobs in the labor force. Statistical data verified the economically corrective force that occurred when minority entrepreneurs transitioned from unemployment to self-employment and contributed to the general economy by paying taxes.

Research that documented failures in education and academic achievement fed into stereotypes that literacy was a great challenge for minorities. Cultural and environmental barriers to academic success existed, but over-emphasizing academic failures often reinforced those failures within the minority community. Foreign-born minorities faced linguistic and literacy challenges that put them at a disadvantage in the workplace. Lack of English language skills limited job opportunities and advancements and dampened entrepreneurial propensity among immigrant minorities. Scholars determined that segregation of minorities leads to increases in poverty, to the decline of neighborhoods, and to social isolation. Researchers posited that when the relative level of education increased, individuals were more likely to leave segregated areas and enter mainstream self-employment.

Education offered formal and informal supportive social structure to business owners. Some of these scholars advocated for education reform to cultivate entrepreneurial intentions. Business education and training courses were fundamental to business ownership. Specifically, the recommendation was for training courses that targeted the two elements of business ownership, courses that increased self-efficacy, and those that improved personal attitude. Researchers recommended business plan courses and skill development exercises for younger minorities. For older minorities, researchers suggested seminars that promoted autonomy.

Two different theories of entrepreneurial empowerment countered the disadvantage theory. First, researchers claimed that business owners created their paths to prosperity. Historians traced the history of modern finance instruments back to Jewish Talmudic law and illustrated the connection between Jewish emigration and the establishment of business communities; Jews left their homelands in pursuit of their entrepreneurial dreams. Second, scholars hypothesized that the deleterious effects of discriminations within the labor-market encouraged minorities to use low-paying jobs as a route to business venture development, and a route to upward social mobility.

Low levels of minority entrepreneurial participation resulted in economic inefficiencies, low levels of innovation, slow job creation, and reduced productivity. Given the economic potential of promoting business development among minorities, researchers needed to address the difficulties associated with business start-up. Development of minority business sector had management, economic, and social implications and understanding the context in which business ownership occurred was necessary for addressing the problems encountered by minorities. There is an urgent need to conduct minority entrepreneurship research in situ (in the world of) and in actu (as it exists).

6
THE THEORY OF RESOURCES

The original work on the resource-based theory (I will abbreviate this as RBT) came from a strategic management specialist, Dr. Jay Barney, in 1991. Dr. Barney added RBT to the strategic management dialogue at a time when researchers sought understanding of the sources of sustained competitive advantage; in other words: What is it that keeps a business going over an extended period of time? Dr. Barney constructed the RBT on the works of researchers like Ricardo in 1817, Porter in 1980, and Nelson and Winter in 1982, who discussed the resource-based view of the company or business. In essence, RBT was adapted to meet the challenges of a modernized, technology-rich business environment. Resource, by definition, is the skill, material, money, or people used to produce an item or service. In the resource-based view, the goal was to determine the economic value of a resource and predict the resource's contribution to the profitability of the company. The resource-based view of the company was the predecessor of the RBT. The key challenge in using this theory to study minority business activity is that Dr. Barney developed this theory to look at big business like Wal-Mart and Sears Roebuck and Company; he was not necessarily focused on mom-and-pop stores or independent contractors.

Until the time of Dr. Barney's development of the RBT, previous scholars analyzed a company's sustained competitive advantage in terms of strengths, weaknesses, opportunities, and threats (SWOT) and the company's externalities. The company's externalities were those things happening outside the business that the owner or manager could not control. The base assumption in the SWOT analysis model was that all companies had similar features and a company gained a competitive advantage by developing strategies around the results of the SWOT analysis. Based on the outcomes of the SWOT analysis, company managers could exploit internal strengths to take advantage of external opportunities. By exploiting internal strengths, company managers and decision makers could find ways to compensate for external threats to circumvented weaknesses that existed within.

The concept of organizational resources as key determinants of business success repeatedly appeared in literature over the past 100 years. The building blocks of RBT came from various fields of study including engineering, philosophy, economics, business administration, and psychology. For example, the work of the engineer, Frederick Winslow Taylor, led to the development of scientific management theory. Similarly, the works of Edward Lorenz, a mathematician and meteorologist, produced complexity and chaos theories. Built on a multidisciplinary foundation, RBT became renowned and widely used in strategic management studies of large companies. RBT had representative elements of evolutionary economic. In evolutionary economics, for example, researchers considered the situational effect of substantive changes in the business environment, or researchers characterized sets of behaviors that could result in long-term competitive advantages. Using simulations, economists determined which practices or mechanisms led to sustainable profitability. Based on the outcomes of these types of simulations, a company could expand and capitalize on practical routines, then discontinue the use of unprofitable ones. As with evolutionary economics, RBT emphasized the complexity of interactions between multiple aspects of business management. To understand why RBT is relevant to small business and minority entrepreneurs requires a deeper discussion.

Dr. Barney developed RBT of the company to create a framework to assess the internal capabilities of a company while accounting for the business environment's direct effect on a company's ability to compete. The variation of a company's internal resources, coupled with manager's use of those resources could create a competitive advantage for the company (or micro-enterprise, in this case). RBT differed from other business management models that assessed the company's functionality within an environment, an environment where all actors possessed the same resources, and where a company's situation differed little from its competitors (e.g., competitive dynamics or contestability theory). The focus was on the unique internal features of the company. The underlying assumptions of the theory were that some resources that a business owner controlled were different and unique when compared to the resources of rivals. In addition, the resources that one business owner controlled could be so unique that competitors could not duplicate them easily.

Business owners who used resources strategically could increase how efficiency their operations ran, overall effectiveness, and could achieve profits. In Dr. Barney's view, business owners and managers needed to focus on two goals. First, using resources to create or acquire a competitive advantage, and second, use the resources to achieve a sustainable competitive advantage. The competitive advantage exists when someone in the business implements a strategy that competing business owners cannot duplicate immediately or easily. In economic terms, a company with a sustainable competitive advantage could remain effective, efficient, and profitable as long as the business environment remained in equilibrium (the same). Sustainability required continual efforts by managers and business owners because all industries were subject to Schumpeterian shocks; economic instability and technological changes could shift a sustainable competitive advantage to a company's competition.

In economic theory, a perfectly competitive business market is one in which all companies have the same capabilities, the same resources, and the same information. In reality, all businesses are different, have heterogeneous or similar capabilities, and information asymmetry is the norm. The RBT encompassed the economic realities of a diverse market. The key point of divergence between RBT and neoclassical economics was the elasticity of supply. In economic theory, as demand increased, price increased; as demand and price increased, supply increased. The time required to increase the amount of a resource could make that resource inelastic; therefore, the resource was likely to produce profits in the short term. Furthermore, as the company develops a resource over time, the inelasticity of the resource (supply) could create a sustained competitive advantage.

Barriers and Resources. Managers' abilities to overcome obstacles to enterprise initialization or enterprise growth depended upon the selected industry and the business environment. For example, financial barriers prevented companies from entering markets that required large amounts of capital or, market-specific resources could be inaccessible to aspiring entrepreneurs. A company's manager is capable of creating a sustainable competitive advantage by bundling and using these distinctive resources effectively. Micro-enterprise managers need to identify potential resources to create a sustainable competitive advantage; then managers need to assess the value, rarity, exclusivity, and nonsubstitutability (see explanation below) of resources. Also, these managers must protect the resources and use their knowledge and management skills to develop resources in ways that created sustainable competitive advantage. Valuable resources have utility and add strength to the organization. Rarity refers to the use of a resource (or a group of resources) in unique ways that contribute to producing profits. Competing companies do not reproduce inimitable resources. A resource is nonsubstitutable if a competitor cannot acquire, or develop a comparable substitute for that resource.

Researchers rarely applied RBT to studies on micro-enterprises. Using RBT to support their argument, one group of researchers tested entrepreneurial capabilities. These researchers found a positive correlation between entrepreneurial capabilities and business outcomes; managers who possessed entrepreneurial skills could sense, select, shape, and synchronize resources to change the competitive environment in favor if the company. However, a key concern was the inexactness of measuring internal resources when applying RBT to studies of micro-enterprises. Applying RBT to studies on micro-enterprises was challenging because of the multidimensional nature of these enterprises and the people who owned or managed them.

7
MINORITY ENTREPRENEURS

Nationally, the average minority population was 27.6% in 2010. According to 2010 U.S. census data, 90% of minority business owners belonged to one of three groups, Blacks, Hispanics, and Asians. The Black population was comprised of African-Americans, Africans, and West Indians. The Asian population included Chinese, Korean, Japanese, Vietnamese, Indians, and Pacific Islanders. Mexicans, South Americans, Cubans, and Central Americans were members of the Hispanic group. According to data from the Department of Homeland Security, approximately 1.5 million legal immigrants added to the racial mix of U.S. residents every year; these data explained the ethnic and racial dispersions of minorities across the country. Although these data showed the cultural mix of the new arrivals, the data did not show settlement patterns. By far, the majority of immigrants settled in major cities along the east coast, and in southern states. Guided by the topic of the world of the entrepreneur and as the entrepreneur exists, the remainder of this book is devoted to the most populous groups of minority entrepreneurs. Scholars often grouped minorities together when studying entrepreneurship; however, census and immigration data shows that there were four distinct minority groups in the United States. There are separate discussions of African-Americans, West Indians, Hispanics, and Asians.

African American Entrepreneurship

The 17th and 18th centuries. Accounts of African American history typically begin with the slave trade. Slavery did not exist in North America in 1619 when the first Africans arrived at Jamestown, Virginia, aboard a Dutch ship. Once the Trans-Atlantic Slave Trade became part of capitalism in America, African slaves endured brutality, family unit destruction, psychological repression, and social reclassification. Consequently, the treatment of peoples of African descent in early America and the antebellum era created numerous political and social barriers.

Historians and scholars called Reconstruction a transformative period for the United States. During the latter half of the 18th century, African American men had a political voice, the same civil rights as European American men, and the freedom to be entrepreneurs. The Civil War ravaged the southern states and consequently, politicians and lawmakers devised methods to normalize Black-White relations between plantation owners and newly freedmen. During Reconstructionists legally sanctioned racial separations and government-supported discrimination reinforced social divisions; Reconstruction soon gave way to Segregation, also known as Jim Crow.

The 19th century. During the 19th century period of Segregation, African American entrepreneurs could not accumulate the resources to participate fully or to compete fairly in a capitalist economy. Quality education, access to capital, and fair housing were accessible by European Americans but legally denied to African Americans. Without full access to all the resources of a capitalist system, few opportunities existed for development, growth, and expansion of African American enterprises. Exclusionary practices limited opportunities, limited loans, and limited access to geographic centers of business. Additionally, exclusionary practices within the labor market tended to concentrate African Americans workers in labor-intensive industries. There were laws that prohibited African Americans from occupations that required reading and writing skills. There were also other laws that denied African Americans the right to file lawsuits against discriminating employers. The rise of discrimination and deepening racism in the United States resulted in the social isolation of African Americans.

Toward the end of the 19th century, geographical patterns of African American entrepreneurship emerged in the United States. Concomitant with ethnic populations migrating to U.S. metropolises in the North and South, entrepreneurs established new businesses. The Negro Business League and its founder, Booker T. Washington, supported and encouraged African Americans to become entrepreneurs. With the backing of the Negro Business League, African American entrepreneurs took advantage of the disadvantages of racism in the South. Segregation pushed African Americans into urban areas, and this concentrated population created opportunities for growth and development of new ethnic enterprises. In southern cities like Atlanta, Birmingham, Durham, and Richmond, African Americans developed businesses, schools, banks, and other institutions to serve their community. In the absence of government support, African Americans used their own economic, institutional, and social capital to build the Black Economy. The Black Economy operated independently of mainstream capitalism. Through these collective efforts, entrepreneurs had opportunities to pursue professional occupations, public service careers, arts and entertainment, and business ventures in southern communities such as Atlanta, New Orleans, and Nashville.

The 20th century. During the first wave of migration from South to North, there was a measurable increase in the number of African American businesses and professional achievements. African Americans migrated from the South during and after Segregation, and newly arrived immigrants moved to the main cities to join their fellow compatriots. Migrations to major cities, coupled with intentional residential segregation led the newly migrated residents to established ethnic enclaves that provided a variety of retail and service businesses for their respective native markets. From 1910 to 1930, the number of ethnic retailers, service providers, and ministers rose sharply in cities like Chicago and New York.

New York City, Los Angeles, and Chicago were examples of older U.S. cities that became hubs for migration and places where ethnic enclaves formed. Within ethnic enclaves, minority entrepreneurs used networking and community organizations as sources of information to compensate for a variety of deficiencies and to learn the business system. In 2011, some researchers indicated that business startups were resource-hungry. Resource acquisition was difficult, sometimes unreliable, and time-consuming; therefore, these community organizations eased the difficulties of understanding rules, regulations, and business systems. Minority entrepreneurs also developed and leveraged political and social relationships to establish their commercial enterprises. Researchers correlated the increase in ethnic professionals with the solidarity that existed in the national consciousness of African Americans at the time; African Americans believed they could exist as a unified entity within an exclusionary capitalist society. The rise of the African American entrepreneur was brief, however. The increase in population in northern cities occurred concomitantly with the demand for services, ethnic products, and ethnic media. However, the rise of entrepreneurship quickly reached a point of saturation in markets such as beauty salons and retailers. Restricted access to professional training and higher education, coupled with the rise of discrimination from European Americans, and the national economic decline of the Great Depression limited the potential expansion of the Black Economy. The Black Economy lost traction and regressed sharply during the Great Depression.

African Americans found innovative ways to sustain their remunerative system, the Black Economy. These innovators created unique and thriving markets for beauty products, and they developed the first national wire service dedicated to ethnic news and interests. In 1935, S. B. Fuller started a business with $25 and went on to build an empire during a time of social and economic upheaval. Fuller, an enterprising entrepreneur, used door-to-door selling techniques to sell ethnic products to ethnic consumers. This novel sales strategy propelled him to become one of the richest African Americans in the 1950s. Fuller was one of the few African Americans who overcame the subculture of institutional and social impediments in American society.

During the post-World War II recovery, African American enterprise growth and development resurged. Challenged by the economic recession and the expansion of large department stores, leaders in the African American beauty industry sought international markets for their products. African Americans legitimized and popularized their products in foreign markets, then reintroduced them to ethnic markets in the United States, a fruitful marketing strategy that emboldened the entrepreneurial community.

The second geographic migratory pattern occurred between 1910 and 1970. More than 6 million African Americans migrated to cities in the North, including Chicago, Detroit, Philadelphia, and New York City. This shift in the population increased racial tensions and instigated intercultural clashes over jobs, housing, schools, and government services. The concentration of African Americans in metropolises created opportunities for ethnic business growth. To meet consumer demands in newly established communities, entrepreneurs continued to develop ethnic businesses such as barbershops and hair salons, publishing companies, entertainment establishments, insurance companies, and retailers.

African American entrepreneurs who migrated to urban areas in the North encountered competition from European American and immigrant business owners. In contrast to the metropolitan experience, immigrants or European Americans often ran businesses in suburban African American communities. Immigrants had the advantage of cultural solidarity, and they experienced less intense discrimination from European Americans. Korean immigrants were particularly astute at capitalizing on opportunities. This ethnic group acquired abandoned neighborhood businesses or established new businesses in predominantly African American communities and succeeded because little competition existed. Korean immigrants were an example of intermediaries who operated from a quasi-monopolistic position. These immigrants exemplified the opportunistic entrepreneurial behaviors that resulted from the rational decisions people made when faced with economic hardship. This group of entrepreneurs typified the Schumpeterian principle; people became innovators and risk takers in response to environmental and economic circumstances. In a world of uncertainty, Korean immigrants demonstrated entrepreneurial superiority; they were the quintessential example of racial minorities who sought opportunities to transcend poverty. Small business ownership offered

Korean immigrants, and immigrants of other countries, individual freedom, and wealth creation opportunities.

Legal decisions in the 1950s and citizen activism of the 1960s challenged the segregation of American society. The resulting Desegregation changed the business environment for African Americans in two ways. First, Desegregation added to the demise of the African American enterprise, making goods that were previously inaccessible to the African American consumer available. This caused erosion of the African American consumer base. In response to this erosion, African American business leaders made concerted efforts to create consumer loyalty within their communities. Business owners often called for boycotts of non-African American businesses; however, boycotts and targeted consumerism were not sufficient to ebb the flow of the African American consumer to large department stores. Second, because of Desegregation, the business environment changed significantly so that several African American-owned companies could make the transition from small businesses to medium-sized enterprises. One example of business growth was the Johnson Products Company founded by George E. Johnson, Sr. Johnson was a protégé of S.B. Fuller, and in 1954, and Johnson started his company with $250. Johnson Products was the first African American company traded on the New York Stock Exchange. In 1976, the Federal Trade Commission (FTC) regulators ruled that Johnson Products had to put safety warnings on some of its products; companies owned by European Americans that manufactured similar products were exempt from the FTC ruling. This single act of discrimination decimated the Johnson Products market share and stock value within two years.

Throughout history, African Americans struggled to participate in a free enterprise system. The researchers cited in this review of the literature showed the discriminatory, economic, and social causes of low levels of business ownership between the 1600s and the late 1960s. Beginning with slavery, through wars and social movements, legal sanctions and discriminations, African American entrepreneurial progress was slow. Despite insurmountable odds, and in the most intolerant of environments, the African American entrepreneurial spirit survived.

The intercultural contact associated with immigration created changes in mainstream society. Acculturation allowed newcomers to adapt to society without cultural erosion but, for some newcomers, it was easier to assimilate into American society. As the society absorbed newcomers, integration, separation, and marginalization processes occurred simultaneously. Then there was the marginalization of minority businesses, claiming that minority businesses had a tendency to be smaller and had lower growth rates. Shelton's research showed that the social structures within particular industries caused stagnation or limited growth of individual minority ventures. Sub-cultures within industries with higher potential for wealth creation exhibited bias against minority entrepreneurs resulting in stratification.

West Indian Entrepreneurs

In America, the most recent phase of West Indian immigration occurred between the 1950s and the 1970s. Emigration changed the consciousness of West Indians, broadened their individual and collective worldviews, yet these newcomers retained their distinct island identities. West Indian immigrant business owners encountered the same cultural and social inequities as African-Americans, but West Indians organized to combat anti-Black sentiments during and after the Civil Rights Movement, thereby assuring their cultural survival. Significant events in African-American history stimulated the development of clubs, churches, and civic organizations within West Indian communities; these groups acted as a buffer between social discriminations and the perception of isolation. Membership in West Indian social networks did not necessarily equate to transactional ease in the business community; these networks required "politicking," or active engagement. Even if the entrepreneurial potential existed at the individual level, the emergence of West Indian business owners would have succumbed to social, economic, and political influences of it were not for the social inter-connectedness. When researchers compared West Indian and African-American business owners, the researchers attributed West Indian success to their distinctive cultural values.

Researchers focused on the assimilation of West Indians to American society and observed how these minorities steered through racial stratification. In the 1960s, two-thirds of black immigrants were from the West Indies or Caribbean nations. Researchers who studied Black issues often grouped West Indians with African-Americans, despite the fact that West Indians consciously differentiated themselves culturally from African-Americans. When institutions attempted to integrate people from different cultures, the attempts often failed or resulted in in-group segregation. It was important for institutions to work individually with cultures, and allow cultures to integrate naturally.

Entrepreneurship in the West Indian culture was a natural phenomenon. An historical investigation of West Indians in the 1800s was a testament to the entrepreneurial fortitude of this minority group. In the 1800s, exiled slaves used wit, wisdom, networking, and other resources to develop formal and informal businesses to secure their newly found freedom and independence. People were trafficking in property, slaves, and commerce entirely in their right. There was an indication that the immigrant entrepreneur's pursuit of business ownership was driven by the need to survive.

When compared to African Americans, West Indians had superior socioeconomic attributes and educational attainments; West Indians were a model minority. For West Indian immigrants who became business owners in the U.S., research showed that the areas of greatest need were education in the American system of business, management of the high costs of business ownership, the willingness to learn, knowledge of accounting, and embracing the need for business investments to affect growth. Programs and policies aimed at supporting West Indian businesses were externally effective but did little to address internal entrepreneurial needs. Researchers attributed policy failings to the policymakers' reliance on institutional economics as a foundation for developing initiatives. The general thought was that institutional-economic theories ignored the influence of culture, racial differences, and informal institutions.

Hispanics Entrepreneurs

Peoples of Hispanic decent were poised to become 25% of the total U.S. population by 2050. There is not much information available on Hispanic entrepreneurship. The variations between Hispanic minority entrepreneurs were by-products of regional social, cultural, and economic circumstance. The entrepreneurial propensity of immigrant Hispanics is attributable to the social climate in their home country. Furthermore, the involvement of family better prepared Hispanics for business ownership; in fact, family support seemed to determine whether the Hispanic entrepreneur initiated the business venture. This group of immigrants was more likely to start new ventures in areas where there was a high Hispanic population.

Researchers developed two theories to explain the propensity for Hispanics to start businesses. The first theory suggested that the presence of an ethnic enclave (business district) provided greater opportunity for business ownership than unemployment alone. The drawback of the ethnic enclave was insulation from other cultures; Hispanic entrepreneurs developed limited strategic relationships with other Hispanic-owned businesses. The second theory suggested that Hispanics chose business ownership because the business environment indirectly supported their entrepreneurship. In Las Vegas, for example, the hospitality industry provided unionized jobs with healthcare and retirement benefits. Using this industry as a support system, spouses of Hispanic workers were more likely to start a business. Researchers determined the prime motivator for Hispanic entrepreneurs was the desire to be independent.

As populations increased in metropolitan areas, there was a likelihood of political and organizational mobilization among Hispanics. Two key determinants in the decision to start a business were the existence of common language and ethnic tastes. Over time, higher Hispanic populations led to assimilation into American society, integration through citizenship, and active military service.

The key disadvantage for Hispanics was less educational attainment. As with other minority groups, foreign education credentials were not readily transferrable to, or accepted by the U.S. The education disadvantage pushed Hispanics into low-paying industries and low-revenue self-employment sectors, resulting in Hispanic over-representation in low-skill industries. In the workplace, Hispanics workers reported experiencing discrimination from non-Hispanic and Hispanic co-workers. The level at which an individual identified with the Hispanic community, and the degree to which the individual networked with the Hispanic community, determined that individual's perception of workplace discrimination. The adaptation process was particularly challenging for immigrant Hispanics in terms of language, negotiating between old and new cultures, and managing anti-immigrant sentiment.

As with all minority groups, Hispanics often took jobs in low-wage sectors, had limited influence in the workplace, and were often ostracized based on language. Marginalized Hispanics frequently turned to self-employment to ease the stresses associated with workplace discrimination. When measured against Whites and African-Americans, Hispanic self-employment rates were lower than Whites, but only slightly above African-Americans.

Asian Entrepreneurs

Through the lens of the disadvantaged theory, researchers claimed there was a Korean small-business phenomenon; Koreans faced several problems in the labor market. The identified problems were language, institutional unfamiliarity, nativism, and workplace discrimination. While the disadvantage theory purported a reactionary rationale for Koreans becoming small business owners, the disadvantaged theory did not account for the cultural propensity for self-employment, and the desire for upward social mobility. Korean collectivism, the value of education and capital resourcefulness were supportive evidence of Korean entrepreneurial ability.

Koreans were perhaps the strongest example of the interrelations between community, economy, and social structures. There was the structural role of ethnic churches as centers of socialization, social networking, and as information conduits. Examining the hiring practices of minority employers proved that minority entrepreneurs hired from within their communities; however, Korean business owners did not always exhibit such nepotism, often hiring Hispanics as low-cost labor.

In terms of the disadvantage theory and minority entrepreneurial success, the Chinese appeared to defy all the premises of the theory. Much of the credit for the success of the Chinese was attributable to their long-term oriented culture. It was said that every Chinese person was a born to be his/her boss, for the Chinese proverb stated, "It is better to be chicken's head than a phoenix's tail." The Chinese placed a high value on fate and luck, and of the two, luck played a greater role in business success than fate did. High levels of entrepreneurial characteristics such as the need for achievement, the desire for high earnings, and the need for family security, both motivated and provided structure for Chinese entrepreneurs. Contrary to Western idealism, the Chinese did not boast their wealth and shunned public recognition of achievements.

Confucianism strongly influenced Chinese traditions and behavioral norms. Two examples, which indirectly related to entrepreneurship, were the values placed on harmony and emotional regulation, and education. The Confucian value of harmony created the interdependent self, which suppressed autonomy and regulated emotions. The second example, Chinese education, students were taught through memorization, and in a system which frowned upon questioning or challenging authority. These two cultural norms channeled the youth toward desiring government jobs, and the culture produced fewer innovators and entrepreneurs. Cultural norms explained why Chinese immigrants pursued niche market opportunities.

In the Chinese language, guanxi was a form of social capital, which referred to relationships or connections between business people. Social capital gave agency to the entrepreneur and ensured business development and business success. The origin of guanxi was in poverty; the poor used their networks to gain access to scarce resources and to create a security net. Scholars used guanxi to explain the propensity for Chinese entrepreneurs to have larger social networks and political association. Immigration created tensions between Chinese traditions and Western individualism; tensions that put traditional values at risk. For example, Western culture threatened filial piety, the practice of holding one's parents and elders in high regard. Filial piety resulted in particular disciplines and behaviors that were socially desirable and culturally acceptable within the Chinese community. Chinese social networks, like family, were non-traditional sources of entrepreneurial support, start-up funding, and human capital.

Not all Chinese entrepreneurs sought start-up capital from their families. Chinese entrepreneurs carefully selected their sources of financing because of the intricate relationship between the funding source and management hierarchy. When the entrepreneur believed that family involvement would be beneficial to the business, then the entrepreneur would ask for family funding and support. In contrast, when the entrepreneur believed that family would interfere with business operations and decisions, financial backing came from others social network members. The Chinese family was a source of emotional support and interpersonal pressure, which provided channels of information that were beneficial to the entrepreneur.

Researchers debated whether the Chinese entrepreneur had business acumen or not. Most Chinese entrepreneurs were not well educated in Western business practices, yet they appeared naturally endowed with business sense. The family was instrumental in the Chinese business, providing much-needed start-up capital, and low-cost human capital. Having family members actively engaged in the business venture had management advantages, and greater trust existed between members. Family members had specific expectations that included increased income and creating an inheritance for the next generation.

The literature on Asian entrepreneurs, when juxtaposed against the disadvantage theory of entrepreneurship, suggested that Chinese and Korean immigrants encountered fewer problems when starting businesses. As discussed earlier, Koreans and the Chinese relied heavily on tight social networks for support. There were inherent problems in the Asian family business. First, family operations exhibited little growth because only a few members were trusted with responsibility. Second, familial relations often turned to favoritism. Third, parental control stifled innovation, and fourth, there were conflicts around the generational control or inheritability of the business. While there were obvious benefits to the family business model, the family could also be deleterious to the business. Guanxi's role in business was simple, business required interactions between people, therefore, and the Chinese entrepreneur's ability to capitalize on business relationships resulted in success. Despite their propensity for entrepreneurship, Asians experienced similar disadvantages of self-employment. For Asian entrepreneurs, unfamiliarity with the legal aspects of business, American business practices, and language were post-immigration problems.

Few researchers looked at (East) Indian entrepreneurs in the U.S. India was second only to China in the number of people who emigrated worldwide. Indian collectivism was a prominent cultural marker, and one that supported entrepreneurial efforts post-immigration; however, Indians also had a greater degree of individualism that allowed faster and broader assimilation into American society. Entrepreneurial success did not depend on enclave communities or an ethnic customer base, in fact, Indian entrepreneurs tended to create businesses outside of their immediate communities. Indian culture, social collectivism, and entrepreneurial characteristics positioned the Indian community to take advantage of policies and programs that supported entrepreneurs. The ease of transfer of education credentials reduced the labor-market disadvantage for Indian. In their homeland, Indians experienced social disadvantage based on caste, religion, and state, but research was not clear on the extent to which social disadvantage affected Indians post-immigration. The primary disadvantage faced by Indians was difficulty expressing their business intentions to institutional representatives in ways that legitimized their requests for capital. Indians were adept at using flexibility and adaptability to overcome most of the post immigration hurdles to business startup.

Entrepreneurship Drivers

The Path to Entrepreneurship. Individuals selected different paths to entrepreneurship. Along the economic opportunity path, entrepreneurs followed market forces and trends. On the cultural path, becoming an entrepreneur was the accepted norm. Along the reaction path, entrepreneurship resulted from forces within society, the labor market, or from individuals' internal desires for independence. Regardless of the path chosen to engage in entrepreneurship people acted in their self-interest, used whatever resources were available to them and embraced risk to achieve vertical socioeconomic mobility. African Americans met with multiple challenges in the labor and business environments, but as challenging as entrepreneurship was, entrepreneurship remained a viable option for those who sought mobility, survival, and self-actualization. Taken individually, culture, race, circumstance, or means did not explain the phenomenon of entrepreneurship. The interaction between a committed entrepreneur, available resources, and elements in the business environment gave researchers insight into African Americans' entrepreneurial.

Forms of labor market discrimination. Minorities exited the workforce and entered self-employment because they (minorities) encountered workplace discrimination, wage discrimination, and organizational assimilation of employee's entrepreneurial outputs. Workplace discrimination as conditions in which employers created unfair policies or acted in ways that treated workers differently based on race, gender, or physical characteristics. Organizational leaders' actions and policies harmed workers or created disenchantment within the workplace. On racism in hiring practices, researchers described the extent to which racial discrimination reduced employment probabilities for African Americans, particularly for women. When these researchers analyzed employment data from 1985, they found African American women were 12% less likely to have a full-time job than European American women were; by 2000, African American women almost reached parity. Most of the gains in African American employment had been in the service sector. African American women achieved employment parity because European Americans reached full employment. Consequently, employers had no choice but to supplement their labor forces with ethnic minority employees. The effects of discrimination on overall economic prosperity were the backlash of the economic costs of workplace nepotism. Nepotistic employers incurred higher marginal costs that eventually caused losses in market share to their non-discriminating competitors.

Wage discrimination as the early or downward career mobility of technical workers. Career mobility occurred laterally or vertically, and resulted when managers intentionally manipulated organizational policies to discriminate against African Americans who were at the start of their careers. African Americans experienced high rates of demotion, and frequent movement within organizations. Using the minority vulnerability theory, researchers proved the hypothesis true that meritocratic ideology influenced employer practices. Moreover, these practices concealed racism and discrimination under the guise of universal organizational principles. Downward mobility removed African Americans from privileged positions that could have propelled those employees into upper-level managerial positions. Overall, African American workers tended to earn low wages and failed to advance within companies because of internal organizational policies and structures.

Corporate leaders' influenced wage discrimination because they often discredited the innovative contributions made by employees. Through reverse assimilation, corporate leaders adopted employees' innovations and did not monetarily compensate the employees. In these studies on workplace discrimination, researchers showed workers had limited influence and power within the organization. This topic repeatedly appeared in the literature. Because of these types of discriminatory forces, workers who faced financial uncertainty and those who were unable to advance their careers turned to self-employment to ease the emotional stressors associated with workplace discrimination.

Self-employment. Workers who experienced disadvantages in the labor market became motivated to pursue their business ventures. Employees exited the workforce and entered self-employment for two reasons. The primary cause of workforce exit was the discriminatory acts of employers. Secondarily, when workers failed to advance within organizations, those employees chose self-employment to gain autonomy. The deleterious effects of discrimination within the labor market, coupled with blocked economic opportunities stimulated workers to act in their self-interest.

In a study of African American men, ages 22 to 40, the sustained self-employment rates remained considerably less than the rates among European Americans or Hispanic Americans. This researcher's analysis confirmed correlations between labor market forces, the lack of self-employment experience, and the inability of African Americans to survive as self-employed individuals. Despite the high rates of self-employment entry, African American men tended to return to traditional employment when wage work became available. This was attributed to the short duration of self-employment to the entrepreneurs' lack of business experience and knowledge. Considering these findings, the researcher believed policies changes aimed at increasing and promoting self-employment and business ownership prospects would be more practical than policies targeting the capitalization of ethnic minority businesses. Researchers verified an increase in the number of self-employed individuals after the legal removal of these policies. Notably, there was a limited correlation between self-employment increases and the elimination of affirmative action policies. Some speculated the removal of affirmative action policies decreased the number of jobs available to minorities thus increasing the number of women who pursued self-employment.

8
SOCIAL AND BUSINESS BARRIERS

In a post-racial society, even though barriers to entrepreneurial opportunity no longer legally existed, a subculture of institutional and social barriers continued to affect African Americans entrepreneurial pursuits negatively. Restrained elements of racial discrimination and systematic inequality replaced the historic bigotries of state-sponsored racism. Despite the gradual removal of legal barriers, social and environmental structures continued to plague and impede the growth of African American enterprises. African Americans aspired to business ownership and made modest progress, however, African Americans had to choose between earning substandard wages and taking the risk of self-employment to make a worthy living. In the view of one researcher, ethnic minority business ownership had definite endpoints. First, business ownership was a vehicle for upward mobility. Second, business ownership was a path toward the revitalization of economically depressed neighborhoods. Third, business development and growth were the ultimate solutions to the unemployment woes of a virulent society.

Social stratification had economic effect. Researchers who investigated the economic effect of stratification found people responded to economic insecurity by using their human capital and personal resources to ease the strains of economic decline. In the context of entrepreneurship, social stratification was problematic for owners of nascent enterprises and for experienced business owners who had ambitions to grow their enterprises. From the literature, there emerged two explanations for the social stratification in the United States and researchers used these explanations to justify the relative achievements of different races. In the racialized hierarchy view, researchers measured intelligence and achievement to rank individual races. In the model minority view, researchers claimed certain groups of minorities were capable of using hard work, motivation, academic achievement, entrepreneurial success, and professional status to achieve economic parity. Researchers sought to debunk the popularized hypotheses that justified, reinforced, and rationalized the American system of racial stratification through statistical modeling of minorities' earnings and education. Disparities in earnings potentials were attributed to educational achievement, demographic heterogeneity, and pervasiveness of discrimination. In a concluding discussion of the thick intersectionalities of race, one scholar recommended researchers should turn away from theories of subjugation and turn attention toward understanding the complexities and intricacies of people's associations with racial and gender identities.

Education

The relationship between education and entrepreneurship has been framed differently. First, education bolstered an individual's human capital and was helpful to the entrepreneur for finding solutions to business challenges. Second, education enabled business decision-making. Third, education was a determinant of business performance. Several researchers showed academic and vocational shortcomings limited the entrepreneurial capabilities of all racial minorities. Achieving literacy remained a challenge for racial minorities. Moreover, the extreme emphasis that scholars, researchers, and statisticians put on the low academic achievement served only to reinforce poor education performance.

Researchers exposed the diffuse nature and extent of educational disparities by analyzing the legacy of limited access to the education system. Problems existed at all levels, and educational disparities penetrated many aspects of African American lives. The Civil Rights Movement, affirmative action policies and legal rulings tempered barriers and opened opportunities for African Americans to pursue higher education. Nevertheless, time, political pressures, and citizen activism fully enforced Supreme Court decisions on equality of access to education. The court's correction of historical inequities netted positive social change for African Americans; however, the need for access to higher education remained as well as a need for improved networking within the African American business community. In a study of survivalist entrepreneurship, it was determined that fewer job opportunities and lower advancement rates exist for people who had limited or substandard education. This claim aligned with the conventional wisdom that getting a better education would result in a higher quality of life. For all the economic and technological progress made in the United States over the last 300 years, the battle for African American education equality continued. Substandard education and racial discrimination remained the most commonly cited explanation for low levels of African American entrepreneurial activity.

People who lacked college level education had fewer entrepreneurial aspirations and were less likely to start new ventures. In an exploration of the educational patterns associated with African American entrepreneurial entry using the Panel Study of Entrepreneurial Dynamics data, statisticians indicated more than half of entrepreneurs had some college education, and approximately 25% of African American entrepreneurs had an undergraduate degree. The level of education attainment and the amount of business experience (knowledge capital) were determinants of industry selection and strategic management decisions. Education was supportive of entrepreneurial capabilities insofar as an educated entrepreneur could find, choose, manipulate, and manage internal resources to exploit business opportunities.

Researchers concurred education supported ethnic minority business owners formally and informally. Consequently, researchers recommended education reform to cultivate entrepreneurial intentions among racial minorities. In the view of one researcher, education and training courses focused on business skill development were foundational, empowering, and transformative. Another group of researchers had similar recommendations but cautioned education alone might not be sufficient for entrepreneurial skill development. Instead, these researchers advocated for mentorship and organizational involvement to help ethnic minority business owners transcend economic isolation. The universal predictors such as social and human capital, individual characteristics, and demographics were inextricable from and conclusively linked to the success of minority entrepreneurs.

Enterprise Legitimacy

For the micro-entrepreneur seeking capital for business initialization or expansion, lacking legitimacy was a barrier to capital acquisition. Researchers commonly referred to the legitimacy of an enterprise in terms of social acceptance, cultural alignment, performance history, age, and profitability. When nascent micro-enterprises lacked legitimacy, enterprise owners could not access traditional sources of economic capital. Possessing financial capital would enable managers to maximize the development and acquisition of resources and, in turn, the possession of resources would serve to legitimize micro-enterprises. Institutional barriers had the effect of challenging the legitimacy of a micro-enterprise, impairing managers' abilities to access resources, and putting nascent enterprises on a path of decline and failure. The decision-makers within financial institutions applied the same measures of legitimacy used for large companies on smaller enterprises. Such measures of legitimacy were incompatible with smaller enterprises.

Finance

Access to capital was one of the most crippling factors for entrepreneurs. Entrepreneurship scholars framed their research with the Schumpeterian principle that business initialization and operation demanded the availability of capital for investment in furniture, fixtures, tool, machinery, inventory, and for payroll. Undercapitalized entrepreneurs were slow to start new companies and could fail in the start-up stages of development. Furthermore, African American entrepreneurs who had insufficient personal equity were less likely to accumulate or access the capital needed to start new enterprises.

Banks. Banks and financial institutions accounted for 90% of the debt financing used by small businesses. Using the Survey of Small Business Finances data (a survey sponsored by the Federal Reserve Board), researchers investigated lending trends related to minority enterprises, and specifically, African American enterprises. Lending institutions routinely discriminated against African American entrepreneurs, reducing African Americans' ability to leverage personal wealth to acquire startup and operating capital. African Americans entrepreneurs who applied for loans or credit faced higher denial rates. For those African entrepreneurs who received loans, the loans carried higher interest rates than loans granted to other borrowers. Furthermore, when African American business owners received loans, the loans were smaller in comparison to the loans given to European American business owners. Fear of denial tended to deter African Americans from applying for needed funds. These trends were as true for startup companies as they were for older companies. In the Federal Reserve Board's Survey of Small Business Finances, statistical analysis showed the median age of the company to be 14.3 years. This finding confirmed the results or earlier studies; researchers quantitatively verified African Americans had less access to debt financing.

Loan officers' practices dramatically reduced access to startup capital for African Americans. Bank and credit union officials used preset criteria for judging credit worthiness, criteria that most African Americans failed to meet. Loan officers used rigid financial ratios to determine credit worthiness and remained unwilling to channel or modify financial products to the diverse requirements of the business community. In some cases, loan officers used the business location to disqualify applicants for credit or startup funds. The mismatch between entrepreneurial intentions and predetermined lending criteria of banking institutions was paradoxical. When the U.S. Department of Commerce commissioned research on the capitalization of small business, researchers found nonminority companies received more and larger loans than ethnic minority companies. Because loan rejection rates were three times higher for African Americans than for other small business owners, researchers determined the outlook for African Americans to a poor one; however, the researchers countered with the proposition that African Americans were an untapped economic resource.

The Small Business Administration. Lawmakers established the U.S. Small Business Administration (SBA) in 1953 to protect, assist, and counsel small business owners. Government-sponsored organizations such as the Reconstruction Finance Corporation, the Smaller War Plants Corporation, and the Small Defense Plants Administration were the predecessors of the SBA. Each of these organizations was a government response to a period of American economic hardship, such as the Great Depression and World Wars I and II. Federal and state governments, small business lending institutions, and business organizations like the SBA had the common goal of helping disadvantaged people shift to business ownership. The SBA adapted its functions to service various government initiatives throughout the years. For example, through the Economic Opportunity Act of 1964, the SBA expanded its loan guarantee program to include marginalized business owners who lived in poor neighborhoods and who could not compete in the marketplace. High loan default rates preceded the program's demise in 1984. In a related effort, from 1977 to 1996, SBA administrators oversaw another program called the Minority Enterprise Small Business Investment Company (MESBIC). The leaders, with the intent of revitalizing poorer neighborhoods and boosting microeconomic growth, used MESBIC to target economically distressed areas around the country. The MESBIC program ended after an extended period of negative return on investment, inadequate distribution of resources around the country, and limited innovative business activity.

Since its inception in 1953, the primary goal of the SBA was to facilitate lending to business owners who had limited capital and limited liquidity. When ethnic minority business owners applied for SBA loan guarantees, SBA agents used equity to net worth ratio as part of the determination matrix. SBA agents relied on the same criteria used by lending institutions and thus denied African Americans startup or operating capital. Equity and net worth standards were particularly problematic for African Americans who sought capital from traditional lending institutions or the SBA.

Typically, African Americans were deficient in both equity and net worth. Additionally, the SBA agents offered epigrammatic training programs, but these programs and services were not sufficient to support entrepreneurial success within ethnic minority communities. Researchers used decomposition analysis of SBA loan approval rates and denial rates to verify findings from earlier investigations. The results in this study provided further evidence that patterns of credit rationing were discriminatory.

Lenders used statistical discrimination to judge the merits of loan applicants; statistical discrimination was a process of applying the perception of quality of an applicant based on statistical expectation rather than using the attributes of the applicant to judge the merits of the loan. The researchers questioned whether SBA loan denials resulted from internal (SBA) criteria or if the loan denials related to past discriminations that influenced business owners' management choices. Investigational findings led researchers to promote the reinforcement of public policy to improve antidiscrimination compliance within lending institutions.

Microloans. Although microloan programs were successful around the world, the literature on African Americans' use of microloans was sparse. Investigations of the underutilization of microloans found no probable relationship between loan availability and micro-enterprise initialization in industries with low barriers to entry. Low-barrier industries were defined as markets in which human and financial capital were not determinants of market entry. Loan grantors in the micro lending industry failed to make any noticeable difference for business startups in the United States because disadvantaged business owners did not use the programs. Administrators of microloan programs in the 1990s intended to give impoverished people opportunities to rise from poverty.

Microloan programs became the politically conservative approach to reducing dependency on the dole and became popular because of their success in lesser-developed countries. In the view of Bates et al., administrators of microloans failed to diversify product offerings sufficiently to match the credit needs of entrepreneurs. Furthermore, microloan programs lost traction in the United States because of high transaction costs for the end user. The underutilization of micro lending by micro-entrepreneurs appeared to defy the theoretical construct that the availability of microloans could promote the growth and development of micro-enterprises.

Rotating credit associations. A testament to the ingenuity of West Indians was the use of rotating credit associations. Rotating credit associations, or ROSCAs, were part of the economy in African societies that transferred to the new world during the trans-Atlantic migration in the 17th and 18th centuries. The exact linguistic origin ROSCAs could not be traced, but within each West Indian community the ROSCA had a different name; ROSCAs were called meeting turn in Barbados, and susu in Trinidad.

ROSCAs involved the developing and maintaining social capital, at times through generations. ROSCAs were informal institutions, which were instrumental in capitalizing immigrant businesses, especially where access to traditional institutional capital was limited ROSCAs were advantageous for the West Indian immigrant because there was no complicated paperwork, late fees, or interest, and access to capital through rotating credit associations and the collateral intimate social ties were integral to the establishment and survival of West Indian businesses. Rotating credit associations (ROSCAs) were quintessential examples of social capital; however, ROSCAs were noticeably absent in the African American business community.

ROSCAs were informal institutions that could be instrumental in capitalizing micro-enterprises and were substitutes for traditional institutional capital. The capital side of the ROSCAs functioned as a savings institution that, on a rotating schedule, disbursed large sums to its members. Members knew the disbursement schedule and could plan to use the funds in efficient ways.

There was social side to the ROSCA that involved trust, solidarity, discipline, and being a valued part of society. African Americans lacked the sociocultural inheritance of the ROSCA, yet this informal banking system might have been an alternative solution to the problems of startup and growth capitalization in African American businesses. West Indian and Korean immigrants were examples of ethnic groups who used ROSCAs effectively. Despite the obvious benefits of ROSCAs, these forms of micro financing depended upon the reputation of the borrowers, were forms of predatory lending, and could have non-traditional costs associated with the borrowed funds.

Effects of the Economic Downturn.

Since 2008, and in the aftermath of the Great Recession, managers of financial institutions reduced the availability of credit to all ethnic minority business enterprises. This reduced availability of finance and funding for new ventures was a barrier to economic development. The weakened economy and tighter credit markets slowed the growth of ethnic minority enterprises. Lower employment rates also strained internal sources of operating capital for enterprises that relied on cash flowing from accounts receivable.

Because the U.S. Department of Justice did not enforce fair lending laws, ethnic minority enterprises had to use high-cost consumer credit to stay afloat. Researchers agreed if companies had equal access to financial instruments then minority businesses' survival rates would increase, and businesses would increase hiring rates. Equal access to financial instruments would also increase bank loan proceeds by 20%, allow local economies to thrive, and the number of government contracts procured by ethnic minority enterprises would increase. However, researchers acknowledged these improvements required new policies to create change.

Human and Social Capital

Social researchers provided evidence on the forceful roles of human capital, parental mentoring, and intergenerational family interactions in business start-up and growth. Researchers classified human capital as including higher education, family, civic organizations, churches, and social networks. Human capital served as a set of informal resources for learning the local business system, and as conduits of information.

When analyzing the parental influence on entrepreneurship, the presence of an entrepreneurial parent encouraged the next generation to become business owners. Overall, social researchers and business researchers agreed parental interaction was a precursor to developing the entrepreneurial mindset. The likelihood of human and social capital resource development and mobilization was strongest within ethnic population centers. In a study of entrepreneurial negotiating skills and resource acquisition, researchers showed entrepreneurs could nurture and leverage their community ties and relationships to achieve success. In the context of local economies, the abilities of community leaders to integrate institutional structures with socially and culturally diverse populations determined the degree of economic progress within a given city or metropolis.

Residential segregation affected human and social capital negatively. When politicians and community leaders clustered the poor together crime and other social ills increased, creating situations that fed into negative stereotypes. Residential segregation put ethnic minority entrepreneurs at an economic disadvantage; moreover, residential segregation disenfranchised these entrepreneurs. Opportunity structures offered many advantages for residents, including better schools, less crime, and greater economic opportunities.

The influences of segregation and the limited access to education and finance continued to present challenging barriers for this group. Some challenged the concept of the negative influence of segregation, claiming within African American neighborhoods were the makings of nonconfrontational movements that could uplift the community and challenge the status quo. Segregation led to a backlash of activism, reform, and cultural resistance that ultimately paved the way for educational, political, and social advancement. However, social capital was part of the institutional, cultural, and historical complex that promoted the development of new enterprises.

Resource acquisition was essential to entrepreneurs in their quest to develop new ventures. New venture developers required finance, plant, and materials. Furthermore, new ventures developers needed access to networks, markets, and human capital. However, information asymmetry was a barrier to assembling these resources, and acquiring information could be confusing for the nascent entrepreneur. In essence, leveraging existing relationships and networks could increase the likelihood of venture success. The effective use of social capital in a micro-enterprise related to a manager's ability to leverage social acquaintances to access resources that supported entrepreneurial endeavors.

Scholars who wrote on social capital theory had not identified singular variables, rationales for variable selection, measures of associations, or types of associations related to this form of capital. Nonetheless, the entrepreneurs' ability to leverage social capital had two characteristics. First, entrepreneurs had to make accurate and timely assessments of the business environment, and second, the entrepreneurs had to react to the business environment appropriately.

Considering the dynamic interaction between family and business, one researcher concluded obvious benefits existed in the family business model, but problems were also part of the mix. Families often provided both start-up capital and low-cost human capital for new ventures. Despite the presence of family support, family-run businesses had problems, including low levels of innovation, low-risk tolerance, and tense familial relations, all of which could be deleterious to business growth.

Culture consisted of social patterns that shaped behaviors and culture appeared to play a pivotal role in entrepreneurship. In a global study of 40 countries, researchers concluded culture robustly stimulated entrepreneurship. However, the effect culture had on entrepreneurship varied among ethnic minority groups. In the United States, other researchers confirmed cultural collectivism could support entrepreneurship, but found African Americans lacking the necessary solidarity to support entrepreneurial efforts. Moreover, the quest for individualism, lack of unity in the business community, and poor networking within the African American community perpetuated low levels of self-employment. In consideration of the cultural aspects of entrepreneurship, the culture people shared was not exclusively or sufficiently supportive of the entrepreneur. A people's culture underpinned the development of the entrepreneurial competencies; the nascent entrepreneur needed to acquire habits, routines, and heuristics to achieve success. No particular cultural format existed which fostered entrepreneurship; however, in the same study, these researchers showed the absence of an organizational blueprint promoted creativity, innovation, and success among budding entrepreneurs.

Business Enclaves and the Underground Economy

Since the 1960s, a shift occurred in which scholars selectively probed the urban ethnic neighborhood. Urban neighborhoods needed strong economic bases, housing reinvestments, and new business activity. Beyond the inclusive reference to the ethnic minority, no researchers explicitly discussed the existence of the African American enclave. For immigrants, the ethnic enclave was a place within a community that protected and encouraged ethnic entrepreneurship. The business owners within the enclave provided coethnic services, products, and employment to meet the needs of an ethnically concentrated community.

Entrepreneurs who possessed ethnic knowledge capital could convert that knowledge into opportunity. For these entrepreneurs, enclaves were particularly lucrative and protective to markets. Enclaves were also attractive to nonethnic consumers who sought out unique products. The strength of human and social capital supported the existence and survival of ethnic enclaves.

Despite the surety of having an inbuilt consumer base within the ethnic enclave, micro-enterprise owners tended to have lower revenues and limited opportunities for growth. Researchers determined African American business owners could rely on an ethnic consumer base for survival; however, higher business survival rates were likely for those businesses that broadened their customer base to include multiple ethnicities.

Within established ethnic enclaves, entrepreneurs added new businesses and created new business and social networks. Scholars confirmed racial minorities were likelier to start new ventures in areas with high ethnic populations. Entrepreneurs who established businesses in ethnic minority neighborhoods did so because of discriminatory push factors. Tremendous potential for new business development existed in urban neighborhoods because high ethnic minority populations potentiated opportunity for ethnic commerce.

On the subject of enterprise viability, researchers found an ethnic minority enterprise in an African American neighborhood or enclave had the same likelihood of survival as similar enterprise in any other American neighborhood. Community network members supported the development of enclaves, and in turn, ethnic business owners met the ethnic consumer needs of the community.

The enclave was a business structure that protected entrepreneurs from mainstream competitors, created jobs for community members, and collaterally shielded members of the community from the disadvantages in the mainstream labor market.

Ethnic enclaves had attributes that were attractive to new entrepreneurs. For example, enclaves had an inbuilt customer base, internal sources of business information, and affordable labor. However, failing infrastructure, reallocation of government resources, abandonment by financial institutions, and economic decline were not conducive to the development of small business and restricted enclave development. Also, the ethnic enclave had drawbacks. First, the presence of the enclave tended to insulate ethnic business owners from other cultures and constricted market exposure. Second, entrepreneurs developed fewer cross-cultural strategic relationships with other business owners. Third, even though business enclaves provided an easy path to business ownership, entrepreneurs faced excess competition.

Underground economy. An undetermined number of African American entrepreneurs operated in the underground economy. In the underground economy, transactions occurred in the absence of taxation and regulation, and outside the formal business system. Illicit, illegal, and antisocial transactions took place in the underground economy. These transactions included selling of unregulated and counterfeit goods, human trafficking, and other illegal operations. The insidious nature of the underground economy created difficulties for researchers who sought to develop theoretical constructs. Social interconnectedness and social networking among African Americans promoted the blending of the underground economy and the regulated economy. There was a symbiotic relationship between business owners and the underground economy. The business relationships between members of these two groups required secrecy and had far-reaching costs. For example, African American entrepreneurs missed opportunities to acquire small business loans because they could not disclose all sources of business revenues and incomes. Because of limited capitalization, poor internal management practices (business owners often performed their accounting and acted as their own legal counsel) and social loyalties, African American micro-enterprises often teetered on the edge of disaster.

Policy

People in every society had a genuine interest in promoting ethnic minority business ownership because higher levels of

business ownership potentially reduced poverty, reduced dependency on the dole, and stabilized unemployment. Furthermore, promoting entrepreneurship contributed to economic growth and balanced income inequities. Socioeconomic theorists suggested entrepreneurial development created stability and sustainability within communities affected by economic downturns. Conversely, low levels of entrepreneurial activity had deleterious effects on the rate of a community's economic development. Policymakers used the existing entrepreneurial culture and historical economic trends to formulate policies that could expand and grow the economy. In the view of this pair of researchers, the combination of policy and history shaped the entrepreneurial environment at the local level.

Historical accounts of the entrepreneur and society repeatedly demonstrated the role of government policy in promoting entrepreneurship. However, the goals of policymakers did not necessarily align with those of the entrepreneur. Although policymakers focused on job creation, stimulation of innovation, and economic growth, the entrepreneurs' goals were upward social mobility, independence, and survival.

Policy makers' and entrepreneurs' goals differed when the barriers (gaps) facing micro-enterprise owners in the northeastern U.S. were investigated. Micro-entrepreneurs had capital gaps, asset gaps, transitional gaps, information gaps, as well as gaps in service delivery or institutional capacity. In order to close these gaps, this group of researchers determined program administrators needed to address obstacles that prevented entrepreneurial success by brokering relationships with the Credit Builders Alliance to disseminate information effectively. Additionally, researchers recommended creation and expansion of incentive programs for entrepreneurs including real estate investment programs and developing tax credits.

Looking at the need for policy alignment with entrepreneurs' reemphasized the fact that policies should support entrepreneurial education and the development of entrepreneurial competencies to prepare societies for the future. Scholars and business practitioners used lessons from African American entrepreneurial history, political pressures, legislation, and social movements to clear a path for African American-owned companies to expand. Policy failures were the fault of the policymakers' reliance on institutional economics as a foundation for developing initiatives. Economic theorists frequently ignored the influences of culture, race, and informal institutions on entrepreneurial capabilities. Moreover, there was evidence of policy failure when policymakers targeted business development in saturated markets.

From President Coolidge to President Obama, presidents and their administrations instituted policies targeting ethnic minority neighborhoods, business owners, and enterprises with the intent to spur self-employment, economic growth, and job creation. For example, in 1964 President Johnson declared a war on poverty when he signed the Economic Opportunity Act. During the Jimmy Carter administration, another notable example of the presidential policy was the Community Reinvestment Act (CRA) of 1977, which targeted low-income communities by modifying the effects of banking discriminations on ethnic minority business owners.

In 2012, officials in the U.S. Government Accountability Office (GAO) commissioned a report on the acquisition of government contracts by ethnic minority businesses. Through various policy initiatives, to meet mandated goals, the government officials designated more than $36 billion in contracts for small, ethnic, and minority-owned businesses. In the GAO report, researchers identified and acknowledged the existence of barriers that prevented ethnic business owners from acquiring government contracts. These barriers included access to capital and business owners misunderstanding the federal contracting process; business owners were unable to bundle contracts, and they lacked internal monitoring capabilities. The creators of the GAO report confirmed the findings of an earlier study in which researchers found disparate award processes in assigning local government contracts to ethnic minority entrepreneurs.

On the promotion of minority entrepreneurship, one researcher presented arguments opposing governmental interventionist strategies. The traditional argument that the government had the solutions for combating poverty and disadvantage was a myth. Economic theorists believed investing in the entrepreneur was the solution to society's ills; Shane countered this belief with two facts. First, business startups did not immediately produce jobs, and business startups lacked economic vibrancy. Consequently, when lawmakers and policy writers based new policies on these theories, the resulting entitlement laws, affirmative action regulations, and urban development policies were ineffective. Second, nascent entrepreneurs started their businesses at home with less than $25,000 of personal savings, and the business owners were hopeful to generate $100,000 in the first five years. New businesses of this scale merely acted as substitutes for wage earners.

In the United States, as national wealth increased there were concomitant changes in the business environment that shifted the economy away from agriculture to manufacturing, and then from manufacturing to a service-based economy. Ultimately, the economic evolution had an adverse effect on business startups because as wealth increased and became concentrated to fewer individuals, business startups decreased. Similarly, as wages increased, businesses shifted investment away from workers and into machinery. In turn, aspiring business owners remained in the workforce because earning potential was more lucrative than self-employment. Furthermore, as the use of machinery increased, operations managers decreased the use of general labor and hired highly-trained professionals who would have started businesses of their own. Politicians used government interventionists' strategies such as the Community Reinvestment Act and SBA mandates to target business initialization. These initiatives tended to attract the least capable of entrepreneurs because the unemployed, and workers with a high degree of job dissatisfaction, were the people most likely to start new businesses. Dissatisfied workers and unemployed workers lacked preparedness for the day-to-day rigors of business ownership, nor were they trained to be business managers. New business owners created an average of 7% of jobs each year. Considering the evidence of economic evolution and lackluster job creation in new enterprises, and the inconsistent record of accomplishment of a small number of companies; therefore, policymakers should target entrepreneurs in "high quality, high growth" industries.

Paths forward for developers of entrepreneurship policy included promoting well-funded and innovative entrepreneurship, easing the barriers to business initialization, growth, and success for nascent companies, and promoting and stimulating economic growth among young companies. Targeting policy at the individual level, government officials could achieve more economic growth than working through administratively cumbersome institutions. Policymakers could influence entrepreneurship effectively if their policy initiatives encouraged gradual entry into self-employment. When entrepreneurs adopted measured approaches to self-employment, venture failure would be less devastating to the economy.

Problems Persist.

Concomitant with two decades of liberal immigration policy and the rapid expansion of American cultural diversity from 1950 to 1970, interest in ethnic entrepreneurship research peaked. Researchers explored the ethnocultural, financial and managerial, and institutional challenges associated with ethnic minority business ownership. Business ownership, when used as a vehicle for upward mobility by entrepreneurs, was a path toward the revitalization of economically depressed neighborhoods, and a solution to the unemployment. To alleviate the disjointedness that led to inaccurate portrayals of the current state of ethnic minority entrepreneurship, researchers called for investigations that coalesced research disciplines. In-depth studies are needed on racial minorities to investigate the reality and depth of problems related to business start-up and growth.

This overview indicated that entrepreneurship researchers relied upon statistical data whenever they assessed enterprise success and failure relative to markets, geography, and the characteristics of the business owners. Federal and state-funded researchers published studies showing the demographic and geographic distribution of small businesses. Furthermore, researchers concentrated their investigations of micro-enterprises on "home-based" or "work-at-home-mom" scenarios. Experts in psychology, sociology, management, and economics individually contributed to the growing body of literature, but more recently, researchers advocated for a multidisciplinary approach to coalescing knowledge in entrepreneurship studies. The interconnectedness between motivation and the numerous elements in the business environment remained fragmented and warranted further investigation into entrepreneurial motivations. Scholars and practitioners called for greater understanding of the effect of business structures on business owners because this knowledge was requisite to creating an optimal blend of talent, function, and economic vitality. Questions remained related to the effect of geography on the ethnic minority micro-enterprise.

For African-American, West Indian, Hispanic, and Asian minority entrepreneurs, the combination of social, economic, cultural, and political factors affected each ethnic group differently. Minorities encountered multiple challenges in the labor market, and entrepreneurship, though challenging, provided a path for social mobility and self-actualization. Culture and ethnicity did not completely explain differences in interaction between the entrepreneur and the business environment. If government programs were to be practical in addressing the social discriminations associated with minority businesses, policy makers needed a critical understanding of the social contexts in which minorities functioned. The squandering of human talent in the United States is potentially detrimental to the country's ability to compete globally.

9
THE LESSONS

Gaining a deep understanding of the coping strategies of minority business owners is a problem. Determining how business structures and barriers affect micro-enterprise owners provides evidence of the causes of underrepresentation and low success rates among minorities. The remainder of this chapter highlights and documents the struggles of minorities in Southeast Virginia.

The business owners who participated in the initial investigation graciously took time out of their workdays to responded to interview questions, and made descriptive statements related to their lived experiences

Collectively, business owners' responses to questions resulted in the development of descriptions of the experiences of the group as a whole. These descriptions revealed how the barriers to business initialization, growth, and success. Understanding these shared experiences revealed information that could be useful to aspiring business owners and business regulatory agencies alike. Micro-enterprise owners could learn how to acquire the resources they need to overcome the effect of barriers on their enterprises. Many of these business owners did reveal strategies for reducing the impact of barriers on their enterprises.

Barriers challenged entrepreneurs' efforts and reduced chances of success. Discrimination, lack of regulation enforcement, illegal business activity, access to funding, and limited marketing opportunity were among the barriers that restricted growth opportunities. Micro-entrepreneurs also identified institutional barriers to enterprise start-up including the city departments, the SBA, and state regulatory agencies. Entrepreneurs cited information, funding, and the ability to network with peers as the internal resources crucial to their success as business owners. This group of twenty entrepreneurs also wanted substantive support from agencies and institutions to overcome business barriers.

All businesses from which information was collected met the basic definition of a micro-enterprise; each business owner had a license issued by the city, had fewer than ten employees, and had annual revenues of less than $150,000. Business owners included retailers, medical professionals, and personal service providers; six female and 14 male business owners agreed to share their wisdom. Demographic data collected during the study showed the diversity of the group. The median age range was 40 to 49 years. Education levels varied, however, 85% of business owners attended college previously.

There were six topics that came from the discussions with the business owners. The topics were:
- The effects of barriers on micro-enterprise owners,
- The influences of agencies on micro-enterprise owners,
- Internal and external entrepreneurial resources required for success,
- Agency adaptation to entrepreneurial resource needs,
- The importance of location, and
- The availability of a quality workforce.

What follows are the interpretive results of the interviews.

The Effects of Barriers on Micro-entrepreneurs

Investigating the effects of barriers on enterprise development, growth, and success from the perspectives of micro-entrepreneurs exposed two types of barriers. First, business barriers resulted from interactions between micro-enterprise owners and regulatory agencies. Second, societal forces continued to challenge entrepreneurial progress among African Americans. Business owners' responses to three interview questions addressed the central research question and identified the sources of entrepreneurial barriers. Business owners identified untimely and unnecessary delays acquiring licenses and permits, poor regulation enforcement, illegal business activities, and discrimination as barriers detrimental to business development, growth, and success.

I began the interview asking entrepreneurs to explain why each wanted to start their own business. This interview question elicited responses regarding the financial and nonfinancial drivers of entrepreneurs. Experiencing discrimination was the main nonfinancial motivation cited for pursuing business ownership.

Discrimination was a societal barrier that affected African American micro-enterprises. Although 95% of business owners had multiple motivations for pursuing business ownership, 25% of business owners cited discrimination as a motivating force. Micro-entrepreneurs perceived discrimination as a problem that affected their enterprises negatively. Business owners referred to different sources of discrimination, claiming that the discrimination came from customers, representatives of business regulatory agencies, and peers within industries. Within their narratives, Business owners gave examples of subtle discriminations and systematic inequalities. Regardless of the source, discrimination was not a deterrent. Encountering discrimination motivated 25% of business owners to be self-reliant and persistent.

Business owners were keenly aware of discrimination as an element of the business environment. Speaking to the ubiquitous nature of discrimination, one business owner said, "I don't want to say that it has to do with a lot of race, but in some aspects, I think it's a little harder for minorities to get the business going." Another retailer remarked that discrimination was evident in customers' behaviors. When discussing regulatory agencies, yet another owner described his awareness of shifts in the way agency representatives treated him. During business initialization, he received "respect and equality" initially; however, after establishing his business he concluded, "it's almost any reason and every reason to get rid of you, period!" A third owner perceived discrimination as society's way of questioning his legitimacy as a business owner; nonetheless, this entrepreneur maintained a sense of pride in business ownership, saying, "it is about your credibility." Another business owner's response to discrimination was, "I've always made sure all my necessary paperwork was up to snuff. I made sure I was licensed, had insurance, and so forth." Overall, of the five business owners who brought up the subject of discrimination as a barrier, the perception of discrimination did not deter any of them sufficiently to terminate their business activities. Here is a selection of quotes from business owners:

- I have seen times where just because you look a certain way, or have a certain color, you can have the most beautiful things in your shop, but just because they don't feel like giving their money to you, they go to the other person, who is even higher in price...
- I don't want to say that it has to do with a lot of race, but in some aspects, I think it's a little harder for minorities to get the business going.
- ... as an African American [professional] it seems like when they bring you in, they treat you with a supposed respect and equality, but once you're there, it's almost any reason and every reason to get rid of you, period.
- It's unfair to folks -- like myself, but I guess a lot of big companies feel the same way about the small guys. I've always made sure all my necessary paperwork was up to snuff. I made sure I was licensed, had insurance, and so forth. I've always felt like my work

speaks for itself.

- When you start your own business, it is about your credibility. People think if you have products, they figure "Well, did they fall off the back of a truck?" I got that a lot, and I run a legitimate business; I have a business license and a tax ID number. So, it was to me like an insult but -- at the same time, it motivated me.

The disadvantage theory of entrepreneurship was based on a cultural hypothesis that included the legacy of slavery, social individualism, lack of business solidarity, and limited networking among minorities. Differences in entrepreneurial capabilities were race-based, and culture created the problems that individual members experienced in the business environment.

The belief was that the internal culture of minorities was singularly responsible for the challenges facing this group of entrepreneurs. Societal forces restricted access to the resources and assets necessary for enterprise development. Factors limiting entrepreneurial progress included information acquisition and access to funding. Business owners confirmed how access to information and funding limited growth and hampered enterprise start-up. The results of this study dispute the claim that African Americans lacked the cultural solidarity and networking capability to progress as entrepreneurs. Excerpts from Business owners' interviews pointed to a socio-cultural shift towards a cohesive minority business community.

Proving or disproving the existence of discrimination was beyond the reason for this book because the sole intention was to explore management strategies related to the barriers to micro-enterprise initialization and growth. The Business owners themselves determined discrimination and racism to be problematic in the business environment. These business owners believed that the discrimination came from different sources, and its presence continued to plague and retard the growth of their enterprises. Moreover, discriminators questioned the legitimacy of both the enterprise and the business owner. According to researchers, in a post-racial society, even though barriers to entrepreneurial opportunity no longer legally existed, a subculture of institutional and social barriers continued to affect African Americans entrepreneurial pursuits negatively. The increased presence of minorities in the urban area tends to amplify the perceived economic threat to the majority, eliciting discriminatory behaviors towards minorities.

A few words on motivation. The business owners' responses confirmed how the human psyche produced motivators that pushed individuals over the threshold of business conceptualization, on toward venture initialization and growth. Motivations were driving forces or factors that compelled African Americans micro-enterprise owners to integrate knowledge, assets, and resources to build profit-producing enterprises. Family ties and responsibilities, unsatisfying employment experiences, and low wages were push factors cited by the micro-enterprise owners interviewed. When people faced obstacles like discrimination or inadequate wages in the job market, these individuals became entrepreneurs out of necessity. Among entrepreneurs interviewed, the motivational pull factors were flexibility, opportunity to create wealth, legacy creation, and the desire to serve the community. Irrespective of the motives to becoming entrepreneurs, all business owners remained committed to expanding their enterprises. Findings confirmed that micro-enterprise owners were products of the antagonistic motivational forces described by.□

Working with Business-Focused Agencies

Posing a direct inquiry into the barriers micro-enterprise owners encountered when working with business regulatory agencies resulted in some surprising responses. Business owners named agencies local, federal, and state regulatory boards as places where they (micro-enterprise owners) encountered barriers. Business owners reported three problems specifically, (a) delays caused by misdirection or insufficient information, (b) illegal business activity, and (c) agencies' failures to enforce regulations.

Business owners reported experiencing delays when attempting to obtain permits or licenses from regulatory agencies. Acquiring permits and licensing delayed 50% of the entrepreneurs interviewed. Problems included understanding application requirements, interpreting policies, deciphering procedures, following guidelines, understanding taxation laws, and a lack of engineering knowledge. Clerks and agency representatives were unhelpful and failed to provide entrepreneurs with sufficient information to execute processes and procedures efficiently. The failure to provide adequate information impaired entrepreneurs' abilities to complete complex regulatory processes. Entrepreneurs were able to advance their businesses by using available resources like the Internet and seasoned business mentors to overcome these challenges. One woman-business owner described her business mentor as one who

"Well, for one… one of the barriers was basically knowing all the regulations that applied to home health. Because with those regulations, it can be a stumbling block especially for the licensure part. Basically, we had a young lady come out, and she told us exactly what we needed. She was very patient and kind, and she outlined everything. She saw that we had this enthusiasm, this drive to make sure that we had everything lined up and everything correct. So she, in so many words, she basically sat down and held our hands and said "This is what I need from you." And she mapped it out A, B, C, D, and E."

For this group of entrepreneurs, following government procedures was laborious at best; however, inconsistencies in regulations between two or more agencies intensified the difficulties experienced by this group of micro-entrepreneurs. During business initialization, existing commercial buildings required remodeling to meet the functional requirements of new businesses. Entrepreneurs who wanted to make interior and exterior structural changes to buildings needed approval from the city's business regulatory department. Even when micro-entrepreneurs understood requirements, navigating processes required knowledge or training that they did not have. For example, one owner knew the policies and procedures she had to follow but recognized that lacking engineering knowledge delayed her building permits; this salon owner chose to outsource the engineering projects to continue with her business plans. For the owner of a massage therapy business, inconsistencies between the city and state rules and regulations delay his business plans. This entrepreneur found himself trapped between two levels of bureaucracy, and eventually lost an opportunity to launch his business as he planned. The experiences described by these Business owners were indicative of actions that dampened productivity. According to the masseuse, different levels of government did not work well together, and agency representatives could not mitigate "the gray areas."

Nonstandard agency practices created administrative problems for micro-entrepreneurs. The insurance industry was an example of how regulations influenced entrepreneurs. The insurance industry was state regulated, but owner-agents and bonds-persons encountered variances in how localities applied state regulations. As this owner explained, although each locality used standardized state-issued forms, each had varying processing standards. For example, a clerk in one county accepted forms completed by hand, whereas a clerk in another county would accept computer-generated forms only.

Inconsistencies in regulation enforcement acted as barriers and affected entrepreneurs' abilities to operate efficiently. Across the business environment, and within various industries, African American micro-entrepreneurs discussed the existence of illegal business activity and its economic impact. Nine micro-entrepreneurs reported knowing of illegal operations in their industries. Entrepreneurs claimed when regulatory agencies failed to enforce rules and regulations these failures led to the proliferation of unlicensed operators and elicit business activity. For example, an entrepreneur in the transportation industry explained how disparities in regulations between neighboring cities affected his ability to increase revenues. According to this independent taxi driver, regulations in the transportation industry-restricted activities "to some degree." He explained how officials in one locality might enforce regulations fully when in a neighboring locality officials did not. Unequal enforcement resulted in unfair competition and decreased revenues for city-based taxi companies.

A beautician explained how failures in regulation enforcement permitted the proliferation of illegal business activity in her industry. According to the beautician,

> "Especially being a minority business, you know they are a lot of people out here bootlegging that don't have a license [and] that are not legal. They're doing the same thing that I'm doing. They're doing just as good a job, but they do not have their license. They may not have the paperwork to support it. So, a lot of times when you go into these agencies, that's how you're treated. If you've ever heard the term "kittician" a lot of times they are kitchen beauticians who are out here relaxing hair doing weaves and braiding, that you know, at one time had to be regulated, and kitchen beauticians actually make it bad for people who are actually in the business -- actually have the paperwork, actually legitimate. Because there's so many people who are talented but they're not necessarily legitimate. It doesn't make them any less talented that they don't have a license, but it just makes it harder for those of us to move forward in our business plan. When we need an answer to a question, sometimes there's the assumption that you're doing it off the kitchen table."

Illegal operators provided services comparable to those of licensed beauticians, but they (illegal business owners) lacked the "paperwork to support" their activities. A local barber said,

> "Yes, in my particular field, I don't feel that licensed barbers and cosmetologists get enough support from the state and local authorities as far as checking up on unlicensed barbers and making sure that barbers are paying the proper taxes and (attending to the) safety and health of the customers. Because very rarely do they come by and check in on barber shops and beauty salons."

The beauty industry was one example of the underground operating adjacent to the legal economy. The owner of a home health agency offered another example verifying consistency of regulation enforcement was a problem for micro-entrepreneurs across industries.

During the interview with the agency owner, it became clear that regulation enforcement affected both business owners and society. She was a professional providing in-home care services for medical patients. This entrepreneur said that unlicensed caregivers "have it down to a system." In the home healthcare industry, unlicensed operators channeled profits away from legally operating businesses and subjected patients to risk unwittingly. Our conversation highlighted the fact that failure to enforce regulations affected micro-entrepreneurs negatively, but of equal concern was the potentially harmful impact on an unsuspecting public. As this business owner put it,

"We have a lot of people who were supposedly out there providing private home care, and they're getting paid under the table. They are not regulated in any way, and we get it a lot. I see it a lot in the hospital setting, I see people sitting with the client or the patient and basically, they have it down to a system. One lady told me that she accepts checks and they have to be written a certain way -- it was crazy, it was a sign. And then, on the other hand, I overheard her tell the patient's daughter that if her mother got sick or whatever, that don't take her to the doctor. One because she takes her to the doctor then this person (the parent) is in the hospital or nursing home bed and she'll (personal care aide) lose her money. So a lot of times these people don't have their [patients'] families best interests at hand. They're just out there making money. And so the families have to understand that these people are not licensed professionals. These are -- most of the time they are certified nursing assistants, nursing assistants, or even personal care aides that have no nursing background whatsoever. They don't have any kind of degrees or licenses as far as being a registered nurse, or a licensed practical nurse."

Business owners' narratives confirmed the existence of the underground economy acting as a barrier to business growth and success. The underground economy was a place where business transactions occur in the absence of taxation and regulation (under the table). Reviewing discussions on illegal operations, micro-entrepreneurs claimed when regulatory agencies failed to enforce existing regulations they (micro-entrepreneurs) experienced lower revenues and limited growth opportunities. According to the owners interviewed for this book, inadequate regulation enforcement promoted illegal business operations; thus, legitimate enterprises suffered revenue losses and erosion of customer bases. Business owners' narratives attested to the insidious nature of the underground economy. Some researchers believe there to be a symbiotic relationship between legal and illegal operations in the business community; the entrepreneurs here discussed learning their crafts and sourcing information from individuals who operated in the underground economy.

Studying the coping strategies of African American micro-entrepreneurs exposed the management strategies used to counteract the challenges barriers posed to business operations. This group of entrepreneurs shunned discrimination with persistence and perseverance. Entrepreneurs coped with delays by exploiting internal knowledge resources, finding alternate sources of information, and continued to pursue their business goals. Probing this topic led to discussions and descriptions of how the lack of regulatory enforcement affected the business operations of this group.

Investigating how agencies influenced micro-enterprise owners showed that agencies influenced entrepreneurial behaviors and abilities differently.

First, the timeliness of agency response to inquiries affected entrepreneurs' ability to gather information and perform functions necessary to the efficient operation of their enterprises. Second, information accessibility and availability supported entrepreneurs' strategic plans.

Asking entrepreneurs what types of help they received, what kinds of help they needed, and what they learned from their experiences resulted in the following explanations. The overarching perception among entrepreneurs was that interactions with regulatory agencies influenced their businesses by slowing business activity during start-up and growth phases. The time it took agencies to generate responses, process paperwork or give approvals was prohibitive to the business pursuits of micro-enterprise owners.

The burdensome nature of administrative processes and procedures affected 75% of respondents; the remaining 25% of respondents reported no problems with business regulatory agencies during either the initialization or the growth phases of business development. About 30% of business owners had problems with a particular city department, 35% encountered difficulties with state agencies, and 15% had problems with licensing agencies. There were incidents of agency misdirection reported by 50% of entrepreneurs interviewed; Business owners needed structured guidance to complete business initialization processes. Entrepreneurs expressed frustration with the quality of advice they received from agency representatives. The owner of a health food store said, "You don't know where to start--so many different services under one roof and you just keep going from one to the other to find out where you need to be--there's no structure." Another business owner, a pharmacist, sought the assistance of upper-level management to acquire permits to complete construction of his business. He described his experiences when he attempted to get required permits to complete construction of his business. After several trips to the city's compliance division, "finally got to a point where they gave me so many ridiculous reasons why they couldn't give me a permit--I had to seek out the head of the department and ask him to see what he could do."

Encounters with agencies caused shifts in business strategies. For example, a business owner discontinued pursuing government contracts and altered business expansion plans. Presenting proposals for government approval required specialized written communications skills that the owner of a carpet cleaning service did not have. According to him,

"...you get a packet that's like a book, and if every "i" is not dotted or "t" crossed, you can't even submit it because it has to be all done to the minutia. To me it was too much paperwork to get through to try to get certain things like government contracts and stuff. You know, too picky for me, so I just stayed with the local stuff around here."

He had worked with agents at the local office of the SBA to acquire government contracts for his technology business but discontinued efforts after several unsuccessful attempts. This business owner lacked the business resources and strategic partnerships necessary to fulfill all requirements of government contracts. These entrepreneurs expressed disenchantment with SBA agents and contracting processes and chose uncomplicated approaches to growing their enterprises.

Agencies influenced micro-entrepreneurs to become self-reliant. One business owner described his predicament when he attempted to follow both state and local regulations. In this case, mandates within the state laws relating to his micro-enterprise conflicted with local rules and regulations. Regulatory agencies followed a "black and white" rulebook and "they don't operate in the gray areas." The entrepreneur suggested if efficient coordination of interagency rules and regulations existed, then nascent micro-enterprises would start stronger, grow faster, and achieve success. During business start-up, this business owner resorted to collecting information from the business peers and the Internet. Three business owners followed similar paths including the salon owner who said, "Now I do the Google." When asked what help and assistance he needed, another owner responded, "I believe it's the self-help information on the Internet. The information you can get online." One owner advised all aspiring entrepreneurs to "take classes in business management, develop and implement a business plan, go to school and get some type of qualifications. Get into the background of the career field that you're going into." In each case described here, self-reliance was an internal resource useful for moderating the influences of agencies on micro-enterprise development.

Access to information was an internal resource (requirement) essential for meeting the growth and expansion expectations of 90% of the micro-enterprise owners interviewed. The availability of information on regulatory agencies' websites facilitated business operations. Information availability influenced strategic decision making for one owner who said, "I think having the ability to see the different bids that are out there, I didn't have that ability when they first started." She had plans to grow her business by acquiring local and state contracts. Having access to contract information enabled her efforts by enhancing knowledge of competition and bid pricing. For another owner, having access to agency information alerted him to expansion opportunities; he said, "Especially when I was thinking about doing government work because working with the folks in contracting there were opportunities there for small disadvantaged business." There was consensus among African Americans that understanding regulations and requirements simplified operational tasks and strategic planning.

For those entrepreneurs who experienced positive outcomes from agency interactions, each had a business mentor or an agency liaison that facilitated processes, assisted with applications, and interpreted regulations.

Entrepreneurs reported satisfaction with the adequacy and usefulness of web-based resources to support their business activity. These findings support the concept that mentor-novice relationships supported entrepreneurial learning and development of the management skills in new enterprises.

Entrepreneurial Resources Required for Success

Determining the skills, knowledge, and resources that micro-entrepreneurs needed to succeed, permitted the development of understanding the uses of human and social capital among the group. Additionally, findings associated with motivation provided examples of opportunistic and survivalist entrepreneurial behaviors. These interviews with men and women aided in constructing a perspective of the world of these micro-enterprise owners and enriched the descriptions of their needs.

Investigating entrepreneurial drivers provided insight to the world of the micro-entrepreneurs. Each entrepreneur described multiple motivators. The desire for independence occurred in 75% of responses and seeking wealth occurred in 35% of responses. Self-fulfillment, family circumstances, social forces, and cultural ideologies were motivators that overlapped wealth-seeking and independence. These excerpts showed the variety of entrepreneurial drivers among micro-enterprise. Responses included "I like doing things my way" and "probably for the flexibility," and "The reason why I started my own business was due to a lot of racism." The second response was indicative of the psychological drive to gain respect. The motivation reflected the same cultural ideology that once united the African American community and supported the remunerative system known as the Black Economy. Some comments included:

- I like doing things my way and that's the reason why.
- Freedom of being in charge of my own life. Making my own choices.
- Probably for the flexibility, freedom and I think it gives you the most control of your income possibilities.
- My own business? More flexibility. Use my gifts and talents to be creative. Benefits with raising kids, more opportunity more time for family.
- The reason why started my own business was due to a lot of racism. When I say this to the fact is that a lot of... not being racists... a lot of Koreans came in selling African-American products.
- I wanted to run my own business after was reading some books by Marcus Garvey and some other authors that mentioned that African-Americans should own their own business [or] try to own their own business and become independent.

Comments like those quoted here exemplified the fact that people selected different paths to entrepreneurship. Similarly, a positive relationship between entrepreneurial intent and the proactive behaviors that led people to start businesses was obvious.

As with motivation, understanding a manager's business growth plan was requisite to understanding the needs of African American micro-entrepreneurs in this study. Considering the future orientation of the group indicated business owners were enthusiastic about growth and expansion opportunities for their businesses. In this group, 60% of business owners had immediate expansion plans, 15% of the Business owners were in the process of developing succession plans so they could retire in a few years. There was no singularity to business growth plans. Business owners had goals that overlapped. Goals included improving customer service, giving back to the community, and mentoring aspiring entrepreneurs. The responses of entrepreneurs included "well right now [pause] the main plan is just to continue to grow the business--the main thing is right now is to put [name of business] on the map to make my business a permanent fixture in the community." The owner of a cleaning service wanted to expand her facility so that she could diversify her business offerings; she said, "I would love for us to have a nice building somewhere." The pharmacist envisioned increasing revenues through e-business; he followed a mantra, which he repeated three times in his interview, "good price, good quality, and good service!" For one owner, business growth meant increased freedom; according to him, "The plan for my business right now is I would like to be able to just work my business and not have another job." The business owners' responses demonstrated the willingness of this group of micro-entrepreneurs to use their resources to build sustainable, profit-producing enterprises.

There were some interesting responses from business owners regarding their perceived resource needs. During interviews, 85 % of business owners considered knowledge an indispensable resource. Entrepreneurs identified networking as a critical component for developing strategic business plans.

Knowledge resources included accessing regulatory information on the Internet, web searches related to planned business activities, and self-education. The cited examples of knowledge found on the Internet included product information, niche market discovery, rules and regulations, and technology. Business owners credited their experiences positive interactions with business agencies (SBA or city offices) to developing working relationships with agency liaisons and industry mentors. In 30% of cases when entrepreneurs made inquiries at agencies, agency representatives redirected entrepreneurs to Internet directly. One had summative advice for all business owners, "Basically, I tell people you need to read, always constantly read, always keep up. You have to keep growing and learning and expanding, and never think you know it all. Because once you think you know it all, that's where you make a fall." This owner considered education and knowledge foundational, empowering, and transformational.

Business owners recognized networking with the business community as a powerful and an authoritative resource often underutilized by business owners. He discussed his observations of how Asian Americans and Hispanic Americans supported their respective ethnic groups in business, and hoped that African Americans would follow suit. According to another business owner, networking could open access to bigger markets or could create opportunities for improving branding. The views of these two Business owners coupled with the following excerpts reinforced researchers claim that entrepreneurs could use social capital to overcome business barriers and achieve success. Business owners who advocated the use of social capital stated, "Entrepreneurs who became members of networking groups added to their social capital, developed joint interests, received mutual support, and acquired reciprocal benefits."

Entrepreneurs needed to protect their resources and use their knowledge capital and management skills to augment internal resources in ways that created sustainable competitive advantages. When asked, business owners supported the notion that resources had an intrinsic value from which entrepreneurs derived utility to strengthen their enterprises. Entrepreneurial success depended upon developing internal strengths and capabilities to cope with, navigate through, or circumvent barriers within the business environment. The narratives of Business owners echoed the tenets of Barney's RBT. Entrepreneurs developed strategies to overcome the negative effects of barriers and created competitive advantages with efficient resource utility and knowledge capital. Narratives confirmed the positive relationship between entrepreneurial capabilities and business outcomes. The business owners possessed entrepreneurial skills useful for sensing, selecting, shaping, and synchronizing their resources to change the competitive environment in favor of their enterprises.

Agency Adaptation to Entrepreneurial Needs

The topic of agency adaptation to meet entrepreneurial needs was one of the questions asked of this group. Business owners' perceived needs included expansion of agency support offerings, affordable access to marketing, access to minority development programs, and financial support for operations. Business owners explained their views on ways that business support agencies could adapt to meet the needs of the African American business community.

According to business owners, meeting business growth goals required supportive services from regulatory agencies. One owner described direct agency contact as "face-to-face" time with knowledgeable agents who could give guidance and information. Micro-entrepreneurs believed face-to-face contact with agency representatives improved access government programs and grant opportunities for minority business development. Some excerpts from my conversations with business owners on this topic:

- Well, after actually getting down into the office, after speaking with someone face-to-face, I found that there was enough information. It was better than speaking to someone on the phone.
- The Small Business Association that's in [city], they're pretty helpful. I think they've got a lot of information out there ... if they expand more and be more available for appointments, just maybe have more workers.
- Well they [entrepreneurs] can go through the SBA now. They have a good local one. I contacted them, and they're always having seminars on how to get government contracts, how to develop a business, the whole 9 yards. So go to the SBA, they have a local office in [city], just go on site, go on the website, and they can really help them out. They're really reaching out now to do that for small business owners.
- Actually, I looked for help with the SBA, looking for classes to help me with the business. I went to a few, but they weren't that much help because they [agency representatives] told you to look online. They give you forms to follow, and that's basically all I got from them. Actually, most of the things that I did, I did on my own, from my business plan to finding vendors. Basically, yeah, I did it on my own.

Business owners referenced resources like the state-sponsored agencies that supported minority enterprises and the online e-procurement system, federal Small Business Administration loan guarantees, matching business investment grants offered by the city, and the national nonprofit organizations. Six business owners referenced the SBA; 60% of these business owners had unfavorable encounters with the agency, twenty % had favorable encounters, and 20% had mixed reviews. Mixed reviews came from a massage therapist who considered the SBA a valuable source of information but commented that understaffing at the local office was a problem. She recommended scheduling seminars and workshops outside of regular business hours to accommodate entrepreneurs who were working during the day. Entrepreneurs who were in the beginning stages of business development could have increased access to services and information. Statements from business owners showed the need for and perceived value of agency support. The owner of a home health agency advised entrepreneurs to be proactive and conduct business transactions with agencies in person saying, "They don't necessarily give you that personal touch because you're just a voice on the phone."

When asked to explain their resource needs, 65% of business owners referred to government programs. A micro-entrepreneur with 15 years of experience believed support from city officials could improve promotion of business activity among minorities. Three of the business owners gave examples of existing programs from which they garnered support. One woman was a member of a local, city-sponsored organization that met each month. According to her, organizers of a local business organization invited guest speakers from city services like the police department, local lending institutions, and members of the business community to share information. Business owners agreed programs, like those discussed here, were beneficial to businesses throughout the city.

Business owners' reports of their experiences confirmed researchers' views that resource acquisition was essential to entrepreneurs during new business development. Business owners' narratives exposed weaknesses inconsistency and continuity of information disseminated by regulatory and business support agencies. When it comes to the utilization of agency support services and resources, 27% to 30% of entrepreneurs used these resources or sought help from business support agencies. Business owners cited difficulty accessing support services because of work schedule conflicts and staffing inadequacies at agencies.

There were differences between the goals of policymakers and minority entrepreneurs. Policies formulated using economic trends failed to align with entrepreneurial goals. Agency managers adapted service functions to suit various government initiatives rather than conform to the needs of micro-entrepreneurs. The goals of policymakers focused on job creation, stimulation of innovation, and broader economic growth while the entrepreneurs' goals were upward social mobility, independence, and survival. Business owners' narratives supported the findings of researchers and affirmed the need for new policies to build a business environment favorable to micro-entrepreneurs. New policies would improve existing systems and meet entrepreneurial needs of the African American business community.

Looking at the relationship between small business and local policies during a period of recession, the role of government in creating an environment conducive to the development of small or micro businesses; however, local policies had greater influence than national macro-policy. The benefits of policies supporting business development centers and marketing programs for micro and small enterprises are confirmable. The views of business owners in this study aligned with two hypotheses. Navigating licensing and permit-granting agencies was a barrier to new and seasoned business owners. Moreover, the availability of funding was an influential factor in business development and growth.

These micro-entrepreneurs recognized the value of marketing for their businesses. Access to marketing and advertising during business initialization was desirable. Although marketing was desirable, affordability was a problem for the entrepreneurs interviewed. A self-employed engineer offered this explanation of the perceived benefits of marketing saying, "I think if I'd gotten some marketing strategy--I would've gotten a lot better." Marketing campaigns were cost-prohibitive for micro-entrepreneurs who participated in this study.

Business owners' discussions of marketing were connected with their discussions of business finance. Acquiring financial support for operations, venture initialization, and growth was a challenge for micro-entrepreneurs. Business owners voiced concerns about managing the risks associated with taking on long-term debt and committing to contract agreements longer than one year. Entrepreneurs who were aware of grant availability and debt-financing options experienced disenchantment with application processes for two reasons. First, entrepreneurs had to pay application fees and work with designated organizations without a guarantee of qualification or fund disbursement. Second, SBA loan guarantees failed to help entrepreneurs access startup funding. Business owners who approached banks for business loans had trouble during the application process or received smaller loans than they required for business initialization or growth.

Business owners were averse to the risks of debt. A massage therapist and life coach wanted financial support that matched her risk tolerance. This micro-entrepreneur expressed interest in a microloan to "test the waters," but seemed unaware of microloan availability. In fact, was the only person in this group who mentioned microloans as an alternative to traditional debt financing. In contrast to the massage therapist, two others tried to access grants and debt instruments to finance their businesses. In both cases, the business owners encountered two problems. First, lending institutions preferred to use personal assets as collateral for business loans. Second, they could only access grants through designated organizations and application requirements included application fees. On the subject of what agencies could do better to help minority business owners, the people interview said:

- From the city, if they had developed a program back then by minorities that were going to open up a new business, they could've shown us how to write a business plan. And taught us some business background, just the fundamentals of being the owner of a business that would've been a great help.
- [There were] things that I needed to be a part of that I wasn't aware of when I first started. Like the Small, Women and Minority [organization]. It was all about just getting to the people and saying, "This is the thing that we can provide to you." Now that posed a lot of challenges. Well, I talked to a lady who actually helps small businesses get started. She directs small businesses to different agencies, companies, and organizations. Things that I needed to be a part of that I wasn't aware of when I first started. -- Being a part of

eVA (Virginia's e-procurement system) which actually allows me to see bids, things that are out there in the community.

- I'm part of the [community name] business association. We meet once a month. The City of Newport News (city representatives) comes once a month, and they address the different situations that are going on in the community. They address activity issues, they address new business issues in town, they address people who are closing down their businesses, and also the City of Newport News business development representative has come to give us information on grants. Grants for your business. You have to fall into the criteria that they have. And this particular group, I can say that they are trying their best. I never saw such a group coming together to help business to know what is available out there. They come and talk to one to one. If you have any concerns about the area that you want to improve, whenever anyone relocates, it's like they have a little bit of everything. And a lot of this information is free. A lot of the follow-up appointments are free. But we have to do the homework. Because nothing comes for free. It's another thing that slows down people. You want to help, but you always have to seek the help. But this particular group in Newport News, I'm telling you, I give them [indicated thumbs up]-- they're great. They're great!

The pharmacist was the only business owner who reported success acquiring SBA loan guarantee. Despite possessing the SBA loan guarantee, lending institutions denied funding. According to this business owner, financing criteria used by lending institutions gave African Americans less access to debt financing. He presented his SBA loan guarantee and funding applications to local and national banks. Despite the value of business assets and the low-risk nature of his business, bank administrators denied all requests for funding. Eventually, the pharmacist signed promissory notes to family and friends to borrow $10,000 to purchase inventory, "I filled out a loan agreement, paid it off, and I'm still here."

A barbershop owner shared his experiences with debt financing and offered advice to the African American business community. When he wanted to expand his business, he went to lending institutions for funding. He found "Some of the banks out here can be biased at times, and they're not willing to give you any kind of hand." With the financial support of a friend, he executed his strategic plan and achieved his goals. However, based on his experiences with lending institutions, he advised minority entrepreneurs to self-finance operations.

One of the most crippling factors for aspiring entrepreneurs was access to capital. Typically, minorities had insufficient personal equity to qualify for loans, and this resulted in undercapitalization of their enterprises. This investigation confirmed that undercapitalized companies were slow to start and likely to fail in the start-up phase. Availability of financing options was a barrier that prevented or delayed business initialization and growth among this group of micro-enterprise owners. Business owners sought assistance from the SBA, city offices, and state organizations; however, none was successful. The entrepreneurs in this study resorted to using personal savings and borrowing from family coffers to finance their ventures.

Location, Location, Location

The old mantra in business is "location, location, location." The city's geographic dimensions presented unique challenges for this group of entrepreneurs. Business owners raised the topic, but views varied regarding the importance of location. For example, having the right location was crucial the clothing retailer who depended on pedestrian traffic and browsing customers to boost revenues. Similarly, for the insurance salesperson, location affected his ability to access his customer base. A retailer of personal care products believed location was a vital resource that he could exploit to grow his distribution network; collaboration was as critical to business growth strategy as customer accessibility was. He wanted to "branch out into a bigger location or headquarters where I can wholesale and do consignments to different African American retailers in the local area." These examples demonstrated business owners' perceived value of business location as a resource.

One business owner perceived location as unimportant. This business owner said that the combination of current technologies and word-of-mouth advertising reduced the importance of location. He believed that today's customers searched for services and products differently. This business owner qualified his view of customers' shopping habits by referencing social media and websites like TripAdvisor®. Rather than focusing on finding an ideal location, this business owner suggested business owners should focus on finding vacant niches to fill with exceptional services or products.

The discussions here provide anecdotal support for the conclusion that business success is directly related to the importance of business location. The unique features of business location and business environment could limit access to economic activity sufficient to sustain an enterprise. As evident in the discussions with minority entrepreneurs, the availability of resources, the business environment, ethnicity, and geography influenced the outcomes of entrepreneurial efforts. For example, local regulatory agencies affected the business environment causing unnecessary and untimely delays when they (micro-entrepreneurs) attempted to start or expand their businesses. This study was narrow in scope; exploration of the relationship between location and business success was limited to the perceptions of business owners. Only the business owners reliant on traffic patterns and population concentrations appeared to agree with these researchers regarding the importance of business location.☐

The Micro-enterprise Workforce

Access to a quality, qualified workforce was brought up by 10% of the business owners. Workforce quality was a resource useful for strengthening the reputation of the business. As a business attribute, workforce quality could improve the business's standing in the community, and allow the business owner to expand service offerings.

When business owners responded to the question about what plans they had for their respective businesses, each relayed their perception of the impact of a quality workforce. The remarks of one owner explained the value of a quality workforce to the community,

"At least that route your somewhat safe. You know the criminal background checks are being done. You know that, on these people, we have Social Security cards and driver's licenses, or state IDs. These are just not anybodies coming off the street with their certificates. Even their licenses, we check those things. Who we send, you best believe that they have been fully checked out, and anytime it's a question we run those type of background checks. If needs be, we can do drug testing and that sort of stuff. A lot of times we require tuberculosis skin tests and we check to see if they had Hepatitis B, but if you get somebody off the street you don't know what kind of diseases or what they're going through, or what they've had. All of that stuff is regulated through our agency."

An entrepreneur specializing in heating and air conditioning services described how lacking a quality workforce decreased his ability to be competitive in the marketplace. According to this business owner, his competitors had more resources and talented employees who were specialists in several areas.

"It's very competitive if you go bid on a [housing] complex or development that they're doing because it's a good old boy network with that. You know, most of the big names like [local company name] and folks like that, they are able to do the heating, plumbing, air conditioning, and so on and so forth. So they can go in and bid, and they can obviously get the work. It's very competitive, and it's time driven because that's how they make their money. They're using one or two guys that have all the skills instead of hiring five or six guys. And it's just easier for them because they have the workforce to throw at it. I don't have the workforce to throw at it to meet those demands."

Because he lacked a stable, talented workforce, he could not acquire large commercial contracts. Frequently, entrepreneurs placed little value on workforce quality; however, as economic conditions improved and as revenues increased entrepreneurs' perceptions of the value of workforce quality increased by 13%. The combination of resources, business environment, ethnicity, and geography influenced the outcomes of entrepreneurial efforts. The narratives of entrepreneurs in this study demonstrated how entrepreneurs engaged the unique features of the business environment.

How people acquire and use human and social capital is a key element of business success. This is the obvious takeaway from business owners who shared their experiences. Investigating the availability of a skilled workforce was beyond the scope of the original investigation and this book. However, the micro-enterprise owners expressed concern about how the lack of a quality workforce limited business growth possibilities. The availability of labor was a barrier to micro-enterprise success and profitability worthy of additional study. In the literature, there were three approaches to studying workforce availability. First, business owners' abilities to access a quality workforce depended upon the availability of an educated workforce. Second, entrepreneurs' workforce needs fluctuated with economic conditions and changed as the size of the enterprise increased or decreased. Third, high ethnic populations acted as sources of affordable labor. These three approaches to studying workforce availability give some clues to solving this problem for micro-entrepreneurs; however, there was little information available about this dynamic, and about African American enterprises specifically.

Human capital included higher education, family, and civic organizations. Each human capital asset served an informal resource for learning the local business system, and as a conduit of information. The perceived experiences of the business owners interviewed for this book confirmed findings of researchers who determined entrepreneurs leveraged existing relationships and social capital to increase the likelihood of business success; this confirmed the utility of social capital and human capital as business resources. Business owners viewed the acquisition of information, knowledge, and the utility of informatics as resources useful for bolstering internal capabilities. Entrepreneurs interviewed in this study explained how these resources helped them to maintain business operations successfully. Information asymmetry was a barrier to assembling resource requirements.

Education alone was not sufficient for developing entrepreneurial talent. The combination of education, social capital, individual characteristics, and demographics were universal predictors linked to entrepreneurial success. Demographic information was collected during the interviews and this depicted the distribution of educational attainments of the study group. Suffice it to say that this information verified the role of education but not the totality of the impact of education on business success.

Business owners identified business networks, entrepreneurial mentors, and agency liaisons as forms of social capital useful for accessing information, comprehending regulations, and generating strategic plans. Entrepreneurs coped with business challenges by using social capital to overcome barriers and achieved success. These entrepreneurs agreed that social capital was part of the institutional, cultural, and historical complex that promoted the development of new enterprises.

Final Thoughts on How to Make Changes

Affecting change was the impetus for bringing this research to the surface instead of burying it in some digital library somewhere. There is much social emphasis on creating positive change. Positive social change is defined as a plan or strategy that has a positive human impact, potentiates social betterment, and is of moral goodness; these are at the core of all social change initiatives. This could include concrete improvements to micro-enterprise management processes, development of strategic relationships with business organizations and institutions, and stimulate changes within the community.

Three things became evident from talking directly with the minorities who have chosen this entrepreneurial path. First, seasoned entrepreneurs can bolster internal resources, expand enterprises, and mentor aspiring entrepreneurs by learning from one another's experiences. Second, new, or aspiring entrepreneurs may use this information to develop internal strategies for managing business initialization processes. Finally, organizations and business support agencies could adjust processes and procedures to meet entrepreneurial resource needs and develop policies conducive to promoting minority business activity. Change may occur if

- Entrepreneurs apply the concepts discussed here to business planning, strategy development and implementation. This may strengthen and support the building of internal resources throughout the lifetime of the business venture.
- Micro-enterprise owners develop and maintain relationships with business network members, mentors, and agency liaisons.
- Micro-entrepreneurs use service offerings of regulatory agencies to bolster their (micro-entrepreneurs') internal resources.
- People use this information to create a business environment conducive to the expansion of the minority business sector.
- People foster a spirit of cooperation between business owners and the community to support minorities who have dreams of business ownership.

The venues for sharing this information include business conferences, networking events, and individualized consultations. These venues are essential to effecting change shat promote economic prosperity among minorities. The recommendations offered here may strengthen the efforts of a determined group of entrepreneurs. These recommendations may also assist in the creation of sustainable enterprises, contribute to job growth, and add resilience to the local economy. Understanding the barriers to business start-up, growth, and success as experienced by micro-enterprise owners is essential knowledge for nascent and experienced entrepreneurs, for agencies that support entrepreneurs, for institutions that regulate industries, and for entrepreneurs who become business mentors. The recommendations for business-owners action are

- Engage local business networks to (a) take advantage of marketing opportunities and (b) create strategic partnerships;
- Actively seek nascent entrepreneurs to mentor; and
- Acquire or build internal resources by soliciting support from regulatory agencies and business support agencies.

On a personal note, I often meet with business owners who talk to me about many of the difficulties discussed in these chapters. My advice to you is do not put off consulting with professionals. You will save a lot of time, headache, and money by working with experts.

ABOUT THE AUTHOR

Dr. Marie Bakari is a professor of Business and Management studies at Strayer University, Newport News. She received her doctorate from Walden University. Dr. Bakari is also a local business owner; she has two businesses currently. Her primary business is IncomeTaxPlus through which she provides accounting, investment, and tax services to business owners and individuals. Additionally, Dr. Bakari operates and editing and coaching service for graduate and doctoral students. Despite her busy schedule, Dr. Bakari finds time for school activities with K-12 students, is an active board member with 2 local non-profit organizations, and is always ready to support local business owners. She is a 22-year resident of this fair city, is married to an historian, Harvey Bakari, and is mother to four.

E-mail: m.bakari@incometaxplus.biz
Website: www. incometaxplus.biz
Address: P.O. Box 14515, Newport News, VA 23608

BIBLIOGRAPHY

Abdelgawad, S. G., Zahra, S. A., Svejenova, S., & Sapienza, H. J. (2013). Strategic leadership and entrepreneurial capability for game change. Journal of Leadership and Organizational Studies (20), p. 394-407. doi:10.1177/1548051813475484

Ahn, T. (2011). Racial differences in self-employment exits. Small Business Economics, 36, 169-186. doi:10.1007/s11187-009-9209-3

Akee, R., & Yuksel, M. (2012). The decreasing effect of skin tone on women's full-time employment. Industrial and Labor Relations Review, 65, 398-426. Retrieved from http://www.ilr.cornell.edu/ilrreview/

Aldrich, H. E., & Yang, T. (2012). Lost in translation: Cultural codes are not blueprints. Strategic Entrepreneurship Journal, 6(1), 1-17. doi:10.1002/sej.1125

Aldridge, J., Medina, J., & Ralphs, R. (2010). The problem of proliferation: Guidelines for improving the security of qualitative data in a digital age. Research Ethics, 6(1), 3-9. doi:10.1177/174701611000600102

Audretsch, D. (2012). Entrepreneurship research. Management Decision, 50, 755-764. doi:10.1108/00251741211227384

Audretsch, D. B. (2009). The entrepreneurial society. The Journal of Technology Transfer, 34, 245-254. doi:10.1007/s10961-008-9101-3

Bakari, M. T. (2014). Barriers to Micro-enterprise Initialization, Growth, and Success (Doctoral dissertation, WALDEN UNIVERSITY).

Bakari, M., & Diala-Nettles, I. (2015). Micro-enterprise Owners: Challenges with Initialization, Growth, and Success.

Bann, C. L. (2009). An innovative view of the entrepreneur through exploration of the lived experience of the entrepreneur in startup of the business. Journal of Business and Economic Studies, 15(2), 62-82. Retrieved from http://www.dowling.edu/jbes

Barney, J. (1991). Firm resources and sustained competitive advantage. Journal of Management, 17, 99-120. doi:10.1177/014920639101700108

Barney, J. (2012). Purchasing, supply chain management and sustained competitive advantage: The relevance of resource-based theory. Journal of Supply Chain Management, 48(2), 3-6. doi:10.1111/j.1745-493x.2012.03265.x

Barney, J. B., Ketchen, D. J., & Wright, M. (2011). The future of resource-based theory: Revitalization or decline? Journal of Management, 37, 1299-1315. doi:10.1177/0149206310391805

Bates, T. (2009). Utilizing affirmative action in public sector procurement as a local economic development strategy. Economic Development Quarterly, 23, 180-192. doi:10.1177/0891242409333549

Bates, T. (2010). Alleviating the financial capital barriers impeding business development in inner cities. Journal of the American Planning Association, 76, 349-362. doi:10.1080/01944363.2010.488717

Bates, T., & Robb, A. (2013). Greater access to capital is needed to unleash the local economic development potential of minority-owned businesses. Economic Development Quarterly, 27, 250-259. doi:10.1177/0891242413477188

Bates, T., Lofstrom, M., & Servon, L. J. (2011). Why have lending programs targeting disadvantaged small business borrowers achieved so little success in the United States? Economic Development Quarterly, 25, 255-266. doi:10.1177/0891242411409206

Bell, S. (2012). The power of ideas: The ideational shaping of the structural power of business: The Power of Ideas. International Studies Quarterly, 56, 661-673. doi:10.1111/j.1468-2478.2012.00743.x

Bernard, H. R. (2013). Social research methods: Qualitative and quantitative approaches. Thousand Oaks, California: Sage.

Bogan, V., & Darity, W. (2008). Culture and entrepreneurship? African American and immigrant self-employment in the United States. Journal of Socio-Economics, 37, 1999-2019. doi:10.1016/j.socec.2007.10.010

Boyd, R. L. (2010). Black retail enterprise and racial segregation in northern cities before the "ghetto." Sociological Perspectives, 53, 397-417. doi:10.1525/sop.2010.53.3.397

Boyd, R. L. (2011). The northern "Black metropolis" of the early twentieth century: A reappraisal. Sociological Inquiry, 81, 88-109. doi:10.1111/j.1475-682X.2010.00359.x

Boyd, R. L. (2012). Race, self-employment, and labor absorption.

American Journal of Economics and Sociology, 71, 639-661. doi:10.1111/j.1536-7150.2012.00825.x

Bozeman, B., Slade, C., & Hirsch, P. (2009). Understanding bureaucracy in health science ethics: Toward a better institutional review board. American Journal of Public Health, 99, 1549-1556. doi:10.2105/AJPH.2008.152389

Brandstätter, H. (2011). Personality aspects of entrepreneurship: A look at five meta-analyses. Personality and Individual Differences, 51, 222-230. doi:10.1016/j.paid.2010.07.007

Candlin, K. (2010). The empire of women: Transient entrepreneurs in the southern Caribbean, 1790-1820. The Journal of Imperial and Commonwealth History, 38, 351-372. doi:10.1080/03086534.2010.503393

Carsrud, A., & Brännback, M. (2011). Entrepreneurial motivations: What do we still need to know? Journal of Small Business Management, 49, 9-26. doi:10.1111/j.1540-627X.2010.00312.x

Carter, W. M. (2012). The Thirteenth Amendment and pro-equality speech. Columbia Law Review, 112, 1855-1881. doi:10.2307/1123631

Casey, C. (2012). Low-wealth minority enterprises and access to financial resources for start-up activities: Do connections matter? Economic Development Quarterly, 26, 252-266. doi:10.1177/0891242412452446

Chang, E. P. C., Memili, E., Chrisman, J. J., Kellermanns, F. W., & Chua, J. H. (2009). Family social capital, venture preparedness, and start-up decisions: A study of Hispanic entrepreneurs in New England. Family Business Review, 22, 279-292. doi:10.1177/0894486509332327

Chao, M. M., Chiu, C., & Lee, J. S. (2010). Asians as the model minority: Implications for US government's policies. Asian Journal of Social Psychology, 13, 44-52. doi:10.1111/j.1467-839X.2010.01299.x

Choi, H. (2010). Religious institutions and ethnic entrepreneurship: The Korean ethnic church as a small business incubator. Economic Development Quarterly, 24, 372-383. doi:10.1177/0891242410375426

Chrysostome, E. (2010). The success factors of necessity immigrant entrepreneurs: In search of a model. Thunderbird International Business Review, 52, 137-152. doi:10.1002/tie.20320

Chrysostome, E., & Arcand, S. (2009). Survival of necessity immigrant entrepreneurs: An exploratory study. Journal of Comparative International Management, 12(2), 3-29. Retrieved from http://www.lib.unb.ca/index.php/JCIM

Chu, H. M., Kara, O., Zhu, X., & Gok, K. (2011). Chinese entrepreneurs: Motivations, success factors, problems, and business-related stress. Journal of Chinese Entrepreneurship, 3, 84-111. doi:10.1108/17561391111144546

Cochrane, P. (2010). African-American entrepreneurial venues and social capital. Journal of Developmental Entrepreneurship, 15, 287-300. doi:10.1142/S1084946710001567

Cohen, D. J., & Crabtree, B. F. (2008). Evaluative criteria for qualitative research in health care: Controversies and recommendations. Annals of Family Medicine, 6, 331-339. doi:10.1370/afm.818

Colwell, K., & Narayanan, V. K. (2010). Foresight in economic development policy: Shaping the institutional context for entrepreneurial innovation. Futures, 42, 295-303. doi:10.1016/j.futures.2009.11.015

Copeland, A. J., & Agosto, D. E. (2012). Diagrams and relational maps: The use of graphic elicitation techniques with interviewing data collection, analysis, and display. International Journal of Qualitative Methods, 11, 513-533. Retrieved from http://www.ualberta.ca

Czymoniewicz-Klippel, M. T., Brijnath, B., & Crockett, B. (2010). Ethics and the promotion of inclusiveness within qualitative research: Case examples from Asia and the Pacific. Qualitative Inquiry, 16, 332-341. doi:10.1177/1077800409358872

Davidson, M. J., Fielden, S. L., & Omar, A. (2010). Black, Asian and minority ethnic female business owners: Discrimination and social support. International Journal of Entrepreneurial Behaviour and Research, 16, 58-80. doi:10.1108/13552551011020072

Dayamin, S. L. (2011). Do minority-owned businesses face a spatial barrier? Measuring neighborhood-level economic activity differences in Philadelphia. Growth and Change, 42, 397-419. Retrieved from http://www.blackwellpublishing.com

Del Campo, R. G., Jacobson, K. J. L., Van Buren, H. J., & Blancero,

D. M. (2011). Comparing immigrant and U.S. born Hispanic business professionals: Insights on discrimination. Cross Cultural Management: An International Journal, 18, 327-350. doi:10.1108/13527601111152851

DeVries, H. P. (2012). Do Indian immigrant entrepreneurs residing in different host countries display the same behavioural patterns? Journal of Enterprising Communities: People and Places in the Global Economy, 6, 138-153. doi:10.1108/17506201211228949

Dworkin, S. L. (2012). Sample size policy for qualitative studies using in-depth interviews. Archives of Sexual Behavior, 41, 1319-1320. doi:10.1007/s10508-012-0016-6

Edelman, L. F., Brush, C. G., Manolova, T. S., & Greene, P. G. (2010). Start-up motivations and growth intentions of minority nascent entrepreneurs. Journal of Small Business Management, 48, 174-196. doi:10.1111/j.1540-627X.2010.00291.x

Ensign, P. C., & Robinson, N. P. (2011). Entrepreneurs because they are immigrants or immigrants because they are entrepreneurs? A critical examination of the relationship between the newcomers and the establishment. Journal of Entrepreneurship, 20, 33-53. doi:10.1177/097135571002000102

Fairchild, G. B. (2010). Intergenerational ethnic enclave influences on the likelihood of being self-employed. Journal of Business Venturing, 25, 290-304. doi:10.1016/j.jbusvent.2008.10.003

Fairlie, R. W. (2013). Entrepreneurship, economic conditions and the great recession. Journal of Economics and Management Strategy, 22, 207-231. Retrieved from http://www.kellogg.northwestern.edu

Fairlie, R. W., & Robb, A. M. (2009). Gender differences in business performance: Evidence from the characteristics of business owners' survey. Small Business Economics, 33, 375-395. doi:10.1007/s11187-009-9207-5

Fairlie, R., & Marion, J. (2010). Affirmative action programs and business ownership among minorities and women. Small Business Economics, 39, 319-339. doi:10.1007/s11187-010-9305-4

Festa, M. M., Wilson, A. J., & Neidermeyer, P. E. (2010). Microlending: What business can do to facilitate community-based growth. Journal of Applied Business Research, 26(6), 11-16. Retrieved from http://www.cluteonline.com

Fielden, S. L., Davidson, M. J., & Makin, P. J. (2000). Barriers encountered during micro and small business start-up in North-West England. Journal of Small Business and Enterprise Development, 7, 295-304. doi:10.1108/EUM0000000006852

Fischer, C. T. (2009). Bracketing in qualitative research: Conceptual and practical matters. Psychotherapy Research, 19, 583-590. doi:10.1080/10503300902798375

Forsey, M. (2010). Ethnography as business owner listening. Ethnography, 11, 558-572. doi:10.1177/1466138110372587

Griffiths, M. D., Kickul, J., & Carsrud, A. L. (2009). Government bureaucracy, transactional impediments, and entrepreneurial intentions. International Small Business Journal, 27, 626-645. doi:10.1177/0266242609338752

Ha, S. E. (2010). The consequences of multiracial contexts on public attitudes toward immigration. Political Research Quarterly, 63, 29-42. doi:10.1177/1065912908325255

Haddix, M. (2009). Black boys can write: Challenging dominant framings of African American adolescent males in literacy research. Journal of Adolescent and Adult Literacy, 53, 341-343. doi:10.1598/JAAL.53.4.8

Hannes, K., Lockwood, C., & Pearson, A. (2010). A comparative analysis of three online appraisal instruments' ability to assess validity in qualitative research. Qualitative Health Research, 20, 1736-1743. doi:10.1177/1049732310378656

Hanushek, E. A., Kain, J. F., & Rivkin, S. G. (2009). New evidence about Brown v. board of education: The complex effects of school racial composition on achievement. Journal of Labor Economics, 27, 349-383. doi:10.1086/600386

Harper, M., & Cole, P. (2012). Member checking: Can benefits be gained similar to group therapy? Qualitative Report, 17, 510-517. Retrieved from http://www.nova.edu

Haynie, J. M., Shepherd, D., Mosakowski, E., & Earley, P. C. (2010). A situated metacognative model of the entrepreneurial mindset. Journal of Business Venturing, 25, 217-229. doi:10.1016/j.jbusvent.2008.10.001

Hays, D. G., & Wood, C. (2011). Infusing qualitative traditions in counseling research designs. Journal of Counseling and

Development, 89, 288-295. doi:10.1002/j.1556-6678.2011.tb00091.x

Heckathorn, D. D. (2011). Comment: Snowball versus respondent-driven sampling. Sociological Methodology, 41, 355-366. doi:10.1111/j.1467-9531.2011.01244.x

Hein, S. F., & Austin, W. J. (2001). Empirical and hermeneutic approaches to phenomenological research in psychology: A comparison. Psychological Methods, 6, 3-17. doi:10.1037//1082-989X.6.1.3

Horn, J. (2011). The founding of English America: Jamestown. Magazine of History, 25(1), 23-29. doi:10.1093/oahmag/oaq003

Hounmenou, C. (2012). Black settlement houses and oppositional consciousness. Journal of Black Studies, 43, 646-666. doi:10.1177/0021934712441203

Hummer, R. A., & Hamilton, E. R. (2010). Race and ethnicity in fragile families. Future of Children, 20, 113-131. doi:10.1353/foc.2010.0003

Hunt, M. R. (2010). Active waiting: Habits and the practice of conducting qualitative research. International Journal of Qualitative Methods, 9, 69-76. Retrieved from http://www.ualberta.ca

Ibrahim, G., & Galt, V. (2011). Explaining ethnic entrepreneurship: An evolutionary economics approach. Thunderbird International Business Review, 20, 607-613. doi:10.1016/j.ibusrev.2011.02.010

Jack, S., Moult, S., Anderson, A. R., & Dodd, S. (2010). An entrepreneurial network evolving: Patterns of change. International Small Business Journal, 28, 315-337. doi:10.1177/0266242610363525

Johnson, C. D., & Eby, L. T. (2011). Evaluating career success of African American males: It's what you know and who you are that matters. Journal of Vocational Behavior, 79, 699-709. doi:10.1016/j.jvb.2011.03.021

Johnson, O. (2010). Assessing Neighborhood Racial Segregation and Macroeconomic Effects in the Education of African Americans. Review of Educational Research, 80(4), 527-575. doi:10.3102/0034654310377210

Kelliher, F., & Reinl, L. (2009). A resource-based view of micro-firm management practice. Journal of Small Business and Enterprise Development, 16, 521-532. doi:10.1108/14626000910977206

Kidane, A., & Harvey, B. H. (2010). Profile of Black entrepreneurs: Identifying factors that discriminate between their levels of success. Review of Business Research, 10(1), 54-64. Retrieved from http://www.iabe.org

Kim, C., & Sakamoto, A. (2010). Have Asian American men achieved labor market parity with White men? American Sociological Review, 75, 934-957. doi:10.1177/0003122410388501

Kirkwood, J. (2009). Motivational factors in a push-pull theory of entrepreneurship. Gender in Management: An International Journal, 24, 346-364. doi:10.1108/17542410910968805

Klitzman, R. (2013). How good does the science have to be in proposals submitted to institutional review boards? An interview study of institutional review board personnel. Clinical Trials, 10(5), 761–766. doi:10.1177/1740774513500080

Kobeissi, N. (2009). Impact of the Community Reinvestment Act on new business start-ups and economic growth in local markets. Journal of Small Business Management, 47, 489-513. doi:10.1111/j.1540-627X.2009.00280.x

Koro-Ljungberg, M. (2010). Validity, responsibility, and aporia. Qualitative Inquiry, 16, 603-610. doi:10.1177/1077800410374034

Kumar, A., & Nevid, J. S. (2010). Acculturation, enculturation, and perceptions of mental disorders in Asian Indian immigrants. Cultural Diversity and Ethnic Minority Psychology, 16, 274-283. doi:10.1037/a0017563

Kuznicki, J. (2009). Never a neutral state: American race relations and government power. Cato Journal, 29, 417-453. Retrieved from http://www.cato.org

Leech, N. L., & Onwuegbuzie, A. J. (2011). Beyond constant comparison qualitative data analysis: Using NVivo. School Psychology Quarterly, 26, 70-84. doi:10.1037/a0022711

Lerner, J. (2010). The future of public efforts to boost entrepreneurship and venture capital. Small Business Economics, 35, 255-264. doi:10.1007/s11187-010-9298-z

Light, I. (1979). Disadvantaged minorities in self-employment. International Journal of Comparative Sociology, 20, 31-45. doi:10.1163/156854279X00157

Liñán, F., Rodríguez-Cohard, J. C., & Rueda-Cantuche, J. M. (2011). Factors affecting entrepreneurial intention levels: A role for education. International Entrepreneurship and Management Journal, 7, 195-218. doi:10.1007/s11365-010-0154-z

Liu, C. Y. (2012). The causes and dynamics of minority entrepreneurial entry. Journal of Developmental Entrepreneurship, 17, 1-23. doi:10.1142/S1084946712500033

Lofstrom, M., Bates, T., & Parker, S. C. (2013). Why are some people more likely to become small-businesses owners than others: Entrepreneurship entry and industry-specific barriers. Journal of Business Venturing. Advance online publication. doi:10.1016/j.jbusvent.2013.01.004

Malti, T., & Buchmann, M. (2010). Socialization and individual antecedents of adolescents' and young adults' moral motivation. Journal of Youth and Adolescence, 39, 138-149. doi:10.1007/s10964-009-9400-5

Marshall, C., & Rossman, G. B. (2006). Designing qualitative research (4th ed.). Thousand Oaks, CA: Sage.

Mason, M. (2010). Sample size and saturation in phd studies using qualitative interviews. Forum: Qualitative Sozialforschung, 11(3), 1-19. Retrieved from http://www.qualitative-research.net

Maxwell, J. A. (2010). Using numbers in qualitative research. Qualitative Inquiry, 16, 475-482. doi:10.1177/1077800410364740

McAndrew, M. (2010). A twentieth-century triangle trade: Selling Black beauty at home and abroad, 1945-1965. Enterprise and Society, 11, 784-810. doi:10.1093/es/khq093

McFarland, C., & McConnell, J. K. (2012). Small business growth during a recession: Local policy implications. Economic Development Quarterly, 27, 102–113. doi:10.1177/0891242412461174

Mijid, N., & Bernasek, A. (2013). Decomposing racial and ethnic differences in small business lending: Evidence of discrimination. Review of Social Economy, 71, 443-473. doi:10.1080/00346764.2012.761751

Miyazaki, A. D., & Taylor, K. A. (2008). Researcher interaction biases and business ethics research: Respondent reactions to researcher characteristics. Journal of Business Ethics, 81, 779-795. doi:10.1007/s10551-007-9547-5

Monahan, M., Shah, A., & Mattare, M. (2011). The road ahead: Micro-enterprise perspectives on success and challenge factors. Journal of Management Policy and Practice, 12, 113-125. Retrieved from www.na-businesspress.com/jmppopen.html

Moustakas, C. E. (1994). Phenomenological research methods. London, UK: Sage.

Mukeredzi, T. (2012). Qualitative data gathering challenges in a politically unstable rural environment: A Zimbabwean experience. International Journal of Qualitative Methods, 11, 1-11. Retrieved from http://www.ualberta.ca

Naudé, W. (2010). Entrepreneurship, developing countries, and development economics: New approaches and insights. Small Business Economics, 34, 1-12. doi:10.1007/s11187-009-9198-2

Ndofor, H. A., & Priem, R. L. (2011). Immigrant entrepreneurs, the ethnic enclave strategy, and venture performance. Journal of Management, 37, 790-818. doi:10.1177/0149206309345020

Nopper, T. K. (2010). Colorblind racism and institutional actors' explanations of Korean immigrant entrepreneurship. Critical Sociology, 36, 65-85. doi:10.1177/0896920509347141

O'Connor, A. (2013). A conceptual framework for entrepreneurship education policy: Meeting government and economic purposes. Journal of Business Venturing, 28, 546-563. doi:10.1016/j.jbusvent.2012.07.003

O'Reilly, M., & Parker, N. (2013). "Unsatisfactory saturation": A critical exploration of the notion of saturated sample sizes in qualitative research. Qualitative Research, 13, 190-197. doi:10.1177/1468794112446106

Obschonka, M., Silbereisen, R. K., & Schmitt-Rodermund, E. (2010). Entrepreneurial intention as developmental outcome. Journal of Vocational Behavior, 77, 63-72. doi:10.1016/j.jvb.2010.02.008

Oswick, C., Fleming, P., & Hanlon, G. (2011). From borrowing to blending: Rethinking the processes of organizational theory building. Academy of Management Review, 36, 318-337. doi:10.5465/AMR.2011.59330932

Pager, D., Bonikowski, B., & Western, B. (2009). Discrimination in a low-wage labor market: A field experiment. American Sociological Review, 74, 777-799. doi:10.1177/000312240907400505

Palys, T., & Atchison, C. (2012). Qualitative research in the digital era: Obstacles and opportunities. International Institute for Qualitative Methodology, 11, 352-367. Retrieved from http://www.ualberta.ca

Perry, N., & Waters, N. M. (2012). Southern suburb/northern city: Black entrepreneurship in segregated Arlington County, Virginia. Urban Geography, 33, 655-674. doi:10.2747/0272-3638.33.5.655

Petty, N. J., Thomson, O. P., & Stew, G. (2012). Ready for a paradigm shift? Part 1: Introducing the philosophy of qualitative research. Manual Therapy, 17, 267-274. doi:10.1016/j.math.2012.03.006

Prabhu, V. P., McGuire, S. J., Drost, E. A., & Kwong, K. K. (2012). Proactive personality and entrepreneurial intent: Is entrepreneurial self-efficacy a mediator or moderator? International Journal of Entrepreneurial Behaviour & Research (18), 559-586. doi:10.1108/13552551211253937

Prasad, A., & Mills, A. J. (2011). Critical management studies and business ethics: A synthesis and three research trajectories for the coming decade. Journal of Business Ethics, 94, 227-237. doi:10.1007/s10551-011-0753-9

Price, M., & Chacko, E. (2009). The mixed embeddedness of ethnic entrepreneurs in a new immigrant gateway. Journal of Immigrant and Refugee Studies, 7, 328-346. doi:10.1080/15562940903150105

Qu, S. Q., & Dumay, J. (2011). The qualitative research interview. Qualitative Research in Accounting & Management, 8, 238-264. doi:10.1108/11766091111162070

Raymond, L., Marchand, M., St-Pierre, J., Cadieux, L., & Labelle, F. (2013). Dimensions of small business performance from the owner-manager's perspective: A re-conceptualization and empirical validation. Entrepreneurship & Regional Development, 25, 468-499. doi:10.1080/08985626.2013.782344

Reskin, B. (2012). The race discrimination system. Annual Review of Sociology, 38(1), 17-35. doi:10.1146/annurev-soc-071811-145508

Rindova, V., Barry, D., & Ketchen, D. J. (2009). Entrepreneuring as emancipation. Academy of Management Review, 34, 477-491. doi:10.5465/AMR.2009.40632647

Sahin, M., Nijkamp, P., & Rietdijk, M. (2009). Cultural diversity and urban innovativeness: Personal and business characteristics of urban migrant entrepreneurs. Innovation, 22, 251-281. doi:10.1080/13511610903354364

Sakamoto, A., Woo, H., & Kim, C. (2010). Does an immigrant background ameliorate racial disadvantage? The socioeconomic attainments of second-generation African Americans. Sociological Forum, 25, 123-146. doi:10.1111/j.1573-7861.2009.01160.x

Schumpeter, J. (1934). The theory of economic development: An inquiry into profits, capital, credit, interest, and the business cycle. New Brunswick, NJ: Transaction Publishers.

Sen, A. K. (2011). Micro-enterprises in inner-city communities: Current challenges and viability. Journal of Business Case Studies, 7, 55-62. Retrieved from http://www.cluteonline.com

Serra, P. (2012). Global businesses "from below": Ethnic entrepreneurs in metropolitan areas [Supplemental material]. Urbani Izziv, 23, 97-106. doi:10.5379/urbani-izziv-en-2012-23-supplement-2-008

Servon, L. J., Fairlie, R. W., Rastello, B., & Seely, A. (2010). The five gaps facing small and microbusiness owners: Evidence from New York City. Economic Development Quarterly, 24, 126-142. doi:10.1177/0891242409354899

Servon, L. J., Visser, M. A., & Fairlie, R. W. (2010). The continuum of capital for small and micro-enterprises. Journal of Developmental Entrepreneurship, 15, 301-323. doi:10.1142/S1084946710001579

Shane, S. (2009). Why encouraging more people to become entrepreneurs is bad public policy. Small Business Economics, 33(2), 141-149. doi:10.1007/s11187-009-9215-5

Sharma, G., & Good, D. (2013). The work of middle managers: Sensemaking and sensegiving for creating positive social change. The Journal of Applied Behavioral Science, 49, 95-122. doi:10.1177/0021886312471375

Sharpton, A. (Producer). (2013, February 21). Keepin it real [Audio podcast]. Retrieved from http://nationalactionnetwork.net/

Shinnar, R. S., Aguilera, M. B., & Lyons, T. S. (2011). Co-ethnic markets: Financial penalty or opportunity? Thunderbird International Business Review, 20, 646-658.

doi:10.1016/j.ibusrev.2011.02.014

Skiba, J. R., Horner, R. H., Chung, C., Rausch, M. K., May, S. L., & Tobin, T. (2011). Race is not neutral: A national investigation of African American and Latino disproportionality in school discipline. School Psychology Review, 40(1), 85-107. Retrieved from http://www.naspoline.org/

Smith, B. R., Matthews, C. H., & Schenkel, M. T. (2009). Differences in entrepreneurial opportunities: The role of tacitness and codification in opportunity identification. Journal of Small Business Management, 47, 38-57. doi:10.1111/j.1540-627X.2008.00261.x

Smith, D. A. (2013). The growth performance of top African American businesses. Management Decision, 51, 163-172. doi:10.1108/00251741311291364

Smith, D. A., & Tang, Z. (2013). The growth performance of top African American businesses. Management Decision, 51, 163-172. doi:10.1108/00251741311291364

Snyder, T. L. (2010). Suicide, slavery, and memory in North America. Journal of American History, 97(1), 39–62. doi:10.2307/jahist/97.1.39

South, S. J., Crowder, K., & Pais, J. (2011). Metropolitan structure and neighborhood attainment: Exploring intermetropolitan variation in racial residential segregation. Demography, 48, 1263-1292. doi:10.1007/s13524-011-0062-z

St-Jean, E. (2012). Mentoring as professional development for novice entrepreneurs: Maximizing the learning: Mentoring as professional development. International Journal of Training and Development, 16, 200-216. doi:10.1111/j.1468-2419.2012.00404.x

Stephan, U., & Uhlaner, L. M. (2010). Performance-based vs. socially supportive culture: A cross-national study of descriptive norms and entrepreneurship. Journal of International Business Studies, 41, 1347-1364. doi:10.1057/jibs.2010.14

Stoffle, B. W., Purcell, T., Stoffle, R. W., Van Vlack, K., Arnett, K., & Minnis, J. (2009). Credit, identity, and resilience in the Bahamas and Barbados. Ethnology, 48, 71-84. Retrieved from http://www.pitt.edu/~ethnolog

Strier, R. (2010). Women, poverty, and the micro-enterprise: Context and discourse. Gender, Work and Organization, 17, 195-218. doi:10.1111/j.1468-0432.2009.00486.x

Stringfellow, L., Shaw, E., & Maclean, M. (2013). Apostasy versus legitimacy: Relational dynamics and routes to resource acquisition in entrepreneurial ventures. International Small Business Journal, 31(3), 1-22. doi:10.1177/0266242612471693

Suri, H. (2011). Purposeful sampling in qualitative research synthesis. Qualitative Research Journal, 11(2), 63-75. doi:10.3316/QRJ1102063

Swift, J. A., & Tischler, V. (2010). Qualitative research in nutrition and dietetics: Getting started. Journal of Human Nutrition and Dietetics, 23, 559-566. doi:10.1111/j.1365-277X.2010.01116.x

Tan, H., Wilson, A., & Olver, I. (2009). Ricoeur's theory of interpretation: An instrument for data interpretation in hermeneutic phenomenology. International Journal of Qualitative Methods, 8, 1-15. Retrieved from http://www.ualberta.ca/

Thomas, O. N., Caldwell, C. H., Faison, N., & Jackson, J. S. (2009). Promoting academic achievement: The role of racial identity in buffering perceptions of teacher discrimination on academic achievement among African American and Caribbean Black adolescents. Journal of Educational Psychology, 101, 420-431. doi:10.1037/a0014578

Tillery, A. B., & Chresfield, M. (2012). Model Blacks or "Ras the exhorter": A quantitative content analysis of Black newspapers' coverage of the first wave of Afro-Caribbean immigration to the United States. Journal of Black Studies, 43, 545-570. doi:10.1177/0021934712439065

Tracy, S. J. (2010). Qualitative quality: Eight "big-tent" criteria for excellent qualitative research. Qualitative Inquiry, 16, 837-851. doi:10.1177/1077800410383121

Turner, D. W. (2010). Qualitative interview design: A practical guide for novice investigators. The Qualitative Report, 15, 754-760. Retrieved from http://www.nova.edu

U.S. Census Bureau (2013a). State and county quickfacts. Retrieved from http://quickfacts.census.gov/qfd/states/51/5156000.html

U.S. Census Bureau (2013b). Race. Retrieved from http://www.census.gov/popluation/race/about/

U.S. Department of Commerce Minority Business Development

Agency (2011). African American-owned business growth and global reach. Retrieved from http://www.mbda.gov/sites/default/files/AfricanAmericanOwn edBusinessGrowthandGlobalReach_Final.pdf

U.S. Government Accountability Office (GAO). (2012). Government contracting: Federal efforts to assist small minority owned businesses (GAO Publication No. 12-873). Retrieved from http://www.gao.gov/assets/650/648985.pdf

Unger, J. M., Rauch, A., Frese, M., & Rosenbusch, N. (2011). Human capital and entrepreneurial success: A meta-analytical review. Journal of Business Venturing, 26, 341-358. doi:10.1016/j.jbusvent.2009.09.004

Van Gelderen, M., Thurik, R., & Patel, P. (2011). Encountered problems and outcome status in nascent entrepreneurship. Journal of Small Business Management, 49, 71-91. doi:10.1111/j.1540-627X.2010.00315.x

Vandermause, R. K., & Fleming, S. E. (2011). Philosophical hermeneutic interviewing. International Journal of Qualitative Methods, 10, 367-377. Retrieved from http://www.ualberta.ca

Virginia Department of Minority Business Enterprise. (2013). Small, women and minority vendor directory [SWaM vendor directory]. Retrieved from http://www.dmbe.virginia.gov/swam_reports/all.html.gz

Walden University. (2012). Center for research quality: Institutional review board for ethical standards in research. Retrieved from http://researchcenter.waldenu.edu/Institutional-Review-Board-for-Ethical-Standards-in-Research.htm

Wang, Q. (2011). African American and Hispanic self-employment in the Charlotte metropolitan area. Southeastern Geographer, 51, 89-109. doi:10.1353/sgo.2011.0007

Wang, Q. (2013). Constructing a multilevel spatial approach in ethnic entrepreneurship studies. International Journal of Entrepreneurial Behaviour and Research, 19, 97-113. doi:10.1108/13552551311299279

Wang, Q., & Walcott, S. (2010). A spatial analysis of ethnic self-employment in metropolitan Atlanta. Southeastern Geographer, 50, 323-345. doi:10.1353/sgo.2010.0001

Wang, R. (2012). Chinese culture and its potential influence on entrepreneurship. International Business Research, 5, 79-90. doi:10.5539/ibr.v5n10p76

Webb, J. W., Bruton, G. D., Tihanyi, L., & Ireland, R. D. (2013). Research on entrepreneurship in the informal economy: Framing a research agenda. Journal of Business Venturing, 28, 598-614. doi:10.1016/j.jbusvent.2012.05.003

Webb, J. W., Morris, M. H., & Pillay, R. (2013). Micro-enterprise growth at the base of the pyramid: A resource-based perspective. Journal of Developmental Entrepreneurship. Advance online publication. doi:10.1142/S108494671350026X

Welter, F., & Smallbone, D. (2011). Institutional perspectives on entrepreneurial behavior in challenging environments. Journal of Small Business Management, 49, 107-125. doi:10.1111/j.1540-627X.2010.00317.x

Wernerfelt, B. (2006). A resource-based view of the firm. Strategic Management Journal, 5, 171-180. doi:10.1002/smj.4250050207

Western, B., Bloome, D., Sosnaud, B., & Tach, L. (2012). Economic insecurity and social stratification. Annual Review of Sociology, 38, 341-359. doi:10.1146/annurev-soc-071811-145434

Williams, N., & Williams, C. C. (2011). Tackling barriers to entrepreneurship in a deprived urban neighbourhood. Local Economy, 26, 30-42. doi:10.1177/0269094210391166

Wilson, G., & Roscigno, V. J. (2010). Race and downward mobility from privileged occupations: African American/White dynamics across the early work-career. Social Science Research, 39(1), 67-77. doi:10.1016/j.ssresearch.2009.03.008

Woldoff, R. A., & Ovadia, S. (2009). Not getting their money's worth: African-American disadvantages in converting income, wealth, and education into residential quality. Urban Affairs Review, 45, 66-91. doi:10.1177/1078087408328947

Woo, H., Sakamoto, A., & Takei, I. (2012). Beyond the shadow of White privilege? The socioeconomic attainments of second generation South Asian Americans. Sociology Mind, 2, 23-33. doi:10.4236/sm.2012.21003

Yang, C., Colarelli, S. M., Han, K., & Page, R. (2011). Start-up and hiring practices of immigrant entrepreneurs: An empirical study from an evolutionary psychological perspective. International Business Review, 20, 636-645. doi:10.1016/j.ibusrev.2011.02.016

Yep, G. A. (2010). Toward the de-subjugation of racially marked knowledges in communication. Southern Communication Journal, 75, 171-175. doi:10.1080/10417941003613263

Yusuf, J.E. (2010). Meeting entrepreneurs' support needs: Are assistance programs effective? Journal of Small Business and Enterprise Development, 17, 294-307. doi:10.1108/14626001011041283

Zhang, J., Soh, P. H., & Wong, P. K. (2011). Direct ties, prior knowledge, and entrepreneurial resource acquisitions in China and Singapore. International Small Business Journal, 29, 170-189. doi:10.1177/0266242610391931

Zhao, H., Seibert, S. E., & Lumpkin, G. T. (2010). The relationship of personality to entrepreneurial intentions and performance: A meta-analytic review. Journal of Management, 36, 381-404. doi:10.1177/0149206309335187